Making Rooms
Your Own

Making Rooms Your Own

Lessons from Interior Designers

New York Social Diary

Sian Ballen and Lesley Hauge   Photography by Jeff Hirsch

Introduction by David Patrick Columbia

RIZZOLI
NEW YORK

New York · Paris · London · Milan

Contents

Introduction

In 2000 Jeff Hirsch and I started the New York Social Diary (NYSD) website. I saw the burgeoning interest in and prospects of the Internet as an opportunity to expand the readership of my column on New York society that ran in *Quest* magazine in the 1990s and then in *Avenue*, where I also served as editor in chief. Within a year we were publishing online five days a week with the Social Diary column and countless pages of party pictures. From there we expanded into columns on social and architectural history, as well as on travel.

In 2006 Sian Ballen proposed that she and Lesley Hauge do a series on interior design, interviewing decorators, and people related to that profession, in their own homes. Jeff and I liked the idea, and he joined them as the photographer. I suggested we name the column "House" and run it on Fridays. The chapters of this book are an extension of that column, inspired by it and presented with NYSD's mixture of inquisitiveness and humor.

The individual strengths of the team are appealing. Sian is an aficionado of the art of interior design. She is knowledgeable and always curious about new and exciting approaches. Lesley, on the other hand, is keenly interested in the individuals: their stories, their likes and dislikes, their opinions and attitudes toward their work. The writers' distinct entrées into each subject give the texts depth, breadth, and intimacy. Interviews were conducted by both women at the subjects' residences. At the same time, Jeff was photographing the interiors with his natural eye for beauty, visual wit, and background details. His visual contribution provides a sense of personality in the physical environments, often including pets, which are an integral and living part of many of these rooms. The results are an opportunity to see and learn about an individual's life in his or her personal spaces.

In the past twelve years, Sian, Lesley, and Jeff have visited, recorded, and photographed more than three hundred people from the world of interior design. It is an interesting and unique world: an important industry in New York, with an enormous financial and social effect on the community. The texts and images in this book allow an intimate look into the domestic lives of thirty-one of these creative personalities. Some stories are revelatory, others inspirational. All offer the simple pleasure of seeing choices made by professionals in the field, in essence how they make their rooms their own. The attraction for this reader—who has only a passing interest in the mechanics of the interior design business but has endless curiosity about lifestyle—is a good, sometimes even exceptional, profile of a creative personage, a way of life, and the decisions made for living lives that are both stylish and efficient. A pleasure all around.

–David Patrick Columbia

Miles Redd

A SENSE OF OCCASION

Above: In the entrance hall, plaster palms set off a table with black-and-white lamps and an oversize mirror. "I like rooms to have cheeky juxtapositions," says Redd. **Opposite:** Black horsehair doors open up to the dining room, where antiqued mirrors are set into panels painted two shades of a chalky green. Redd mixes a dining table of his design with 1960s leather chairs and an eighteenth-century Italian gilt chair.

When Miles Redd invites friends over for a dinner party at his NoHo apartment, he asks them to wear black tie. Some think this is ridiculous, but when they come, they always have a wonderful time, Redd declares, and they always look good in the pictures afterward.

A sense of occasion is something Redd feels we are losing. This sentiment is reflected in his design, where rooms are turned into choreographed settings that encourage a life lived to the fullest. He joyfully sets up creative tension between disparate styles, employing Chinese wallpaper, eighteenth-century furniture, and modern art against a backdrop of saturated color and vibrant fabrics. Redd is fascinated with the eighteenth century as well as with Edwardian England, and admires how such master filmmakers as Ismail Merchant and James Ivory so cleverly render this period in their films, making impermanent sets look so sumptuous. "It's all borrowed and spackled and sort of done on the cheap and yet it doesn't look that way," Redd says.

Film and fashion are equally influential on Redd—he received his first degree in film studies from New York University before studying at Parsons School of Design. He went on to spend ten years as the creative director at Oscar de la Renta. It was a black tie dinner party hosted by the de la Rentas for the collector and philanthropist Jayne Wrightsman that inspires his own soirees. "It was just like something out of *The Age of Innocence*," Redd recalls. He also remembers how he was so intimidated by the assembled company that the hostess, Annette de la Renta, held his hand under the dinner table. Now, many years into a highly successful career that includes working with the likes of both John Rosselli and Bunny Williams, it's unlikely he will ever again be so intimidated.

Redd speaks his mind when it comes to likes and dislikes. He has a particular aversion to roller suitcases, for example ("It's the sound they make. . . . It seems like the end of civilization!"), but loves the idea of painting a door a different color on each side. He also loves the black lacquered ceiling in his kitchen and embraces "a kind of baroque-ness" in his design. "Anyone who makes their business about taste is subjecting themselves to a degree of judgment. [But] I love the things I love . . . and to hell with it!"

Left: Peeking into the living room from the dining room, layers of art, accessories, and thoughtful details distinguish an approach to decorating that is both maximalist and refined.
Below: A brown-and-white striped silk fabric from Clarence House is the backdrop for Swedish antique wall panels and an overmantel mirror mounted with a cartel clock. Bold geometric pillows top a tufted velvet sofa upholstered in a Prelle silk velvet.

Left: In a nod to Frances Elkins, Redd placed a pair of loop chairs in front of the living room fireplace. The portrait in a William Kent–style frame was an auction find, and the French corner chair and ottoman are covered in a Cubist fabric designed by Redd for Schumacher. **Below left:** A bird's-eye view into the rear garden, where a bust of Diana takes center stage. **Below:** A terra-cotta figure stands over the bar table in the corner of the living room. "I always encourage clients to include a bar—it makes the room so inviting."

Above: Doris Duke would have been completely at home in the library, where red chairs from her former movie room take center stage. A flattering pink satin fabric on the walls and a curvaceous Venetian mirror hanging above the faience fireplace mantel combine to give the room a decadent feel. **Right:** Redd knew early on that he "just had to have" these zebra skin doors. Nearby, Leslie Hearn's *Panther* hangs above a copy of an eighteenth-century console by Christopher Hodsoll. **Opposite:** Redd fell in love with the mirrored bed by Serge Roche for Mrs. William Paley. The original, owned by his former employer and friend Bunny Williams, was the inspiration for his version and is upholstered in a blue-and-gray silk stripe.

Q+A

with Miles Redd

In a few words how would you describe your design style?
I love grandeur, but with a cozy, nonchalant air. I love contrast in decorating: high and low, modern and eighteenth century, crumbly and glossy, all punctuated with clean, fresh color.

Name a past designer, artist, or creative who has had the most influence on your style.
In terms of interior design—all roads lead to Annette de la Renta and Furlow Gatewood. Many people have taught me a lot along the way, but Furlow and Annette are the ones who speak directly to my soul.

What would your perfect room look like?
I am moving toward the simplicity and refinement of Hubert de Givenchy in the South of France.

What are some of the design rules you've had to unlearn as you've become more experienced?
Always simplify—it makes things stronger. Elegance is refusal.

What's a design risk worth taking?
Scale—the bigger the better!

What's your best budget-friendly design hack?

Paint the doors a contrasting color to the trim.

Tell us ways that you used lighting to resolve a dark apartment.
Picture lights can do wonders.

How do you make your home feel welcoming?
Dim the lights and light the candles; put on soft music.

What truly gives a home "life"?
Plants and people—one needs life to give life!

How did you design around your pets?
Get hypoallergenic pets!

What's your best way to start the day?
A bath!

What's your weekend routine?
Sleep in, leisurely breakfast, exercise, see a movie, dine with friends, read, and relax.

What do you covet but can't afford?
A John Singer Sargent

Do you wish you could spend more time at home?
Yes!

What job would you be terrible at?
Customer service at Circuit City

What smells of home for you?
Citrus, boxwood, and paperwhites

How long can you go without tidying up?
An hour

Do you have a treasured piece of clothing in your closet?
A pink dinner jacket good friends gave me

How do you make sure you enjoy your own parties?
Hire a good staff that knows what to do, and pretend you are a guest.

How do you subtly let guests know you want them to leave?
Serve coffee and ice water with lemon.

How do you stock a perfect bar?
Think of everything you want to drink and buy it. I copy the ones I have seen in grand English country houses; they have everything from 7UP to Clamato juice.

What is your favorite cocktail?
Gin and tonic

What sort of things do you like to do the "old-fashioned" way?
All things!

What's the worst thing about living in New York?
The cost of living

What small things make a bad New York day better?
Coming home to a nice apartment

What do you hope never changes about New York?
That it gets so expensive, the bright, young things will flock elsewhere.

How do you get around town?
Subway, Citi Bike, cab, Uber

Is there a particular place in the city that has special meaning for you?
I just love roaming all over downtown.

Redd discovered this mirrored bathroom at a salvage warehouse in Lake Forest, Illinois, and had it reinstalled in his town house. The room was rescued from the Lester Armour House in Lake Bluff, which was designed by David Adler.

Garrow Kedigian

STREAMLINED CLASSICISM

Above: The walls of the dining/ music room are upholstered in a quiet pattern and defined by large-scale nailhead trimming. Kedigian selected a high-gloss black from Fine Paints of Europe for the trim. The original display cabinets were reinvigorated with a faux-limestone finish. **Opposite:** A bedside table is arranged with a perfect balance of photographs and found objects collected over the years. "I am an avid shopper of unique objects, and properly layering them is an important aspect of my design approach."

It's possible that the ghost of Fred Astaire dances through Garrow Kedigian's Park Avenue apartment because, only two owners ago, it indeed belonged to the twentieth-century icon. It's the forever apartment that Kedigian promised himself he would have by the time he turned forty: he finished his renovations just in time to throw his fortieth birthday party for 175 people. Of course, it was black tie and Fred Astaire themed. "It was the most fabulous party. We danced, we sang. It was my showcasing of the apartment," Kedigian says.

Kedigian is a designer who sees the beauty in gentle decay. Instead of stripping the aged parquet floors, he had the renovation contractors protect them with Masonite. Wanting to keep something of Astaire's in the apartment, he saved some lengths of original dark-green velvet curtaining to cover a banquette. A new opening was constructed between the library, formerly the master bedroom, and the dining room; the resulting doorway and an existing one were resized to a uniform width, forming an enfilade. People often remark on how "French" his style is, but that's not something he tries to consciously achieve. Perhaps it's just his childhood memories—of summers in Paris with his grandmother—speaking through his work.

Of Armenian descent, Kedigian grew up in Montreal, where he studied architecture at McGill University and still keeps a historic town house. Architectural elements are still his first point of departure when planning an interior, and he relies on his instincts as an accomplished painter when it comes to color. He never does white walls and painstakingly selects unusual colors—old ivory, glossy chestnut, and a luminous Vermeer-like blue—which evoke other eras. The carefully chosen "noncolor" of his paneled living room walls, which he calls "Brown Paper Bag," seems plain, but the hand of the designer shows in the single gilded line within each panel, which gracefully animates the tone.

Rising at 4:30 a.m., Kedigian works from home, which he loves. At the end of a working day, he might make his way to the Tap Room at the University Club or his local favorite, the Mark Restaurant at the Mark Hotel. On Sundays, it's piano practice on the Hazelton grand piano he received as a gift when he was only three years old. "I seem to have been working on 'Clair de Lune' for years now."

Above: The large living room was given an intimate feeling with two seating groupings: one that is cozily angled around the fireplace and another more formal arrangement in the center of the room. The Persian rug was turned to its underside in order to mute the tones—a trick that can instantly lift and brighten a room.
Left: Purchases from the Marché aux Puces: a bronze Greek head and a midcentury modern lamp. **Opposite:** A tufted, brown velvet banquette provides additional seating. Kedigian had a corner of a small Italian painting scanned and enlarged on canvas for a contemporary-in-scale yet traditional work of art. The eighteenth-century Dutch side table is from Evergreen Antiques.

Left: Kedigian knew immediately that he wanted to open the walls between the dining/music room and the adjacent room, extending the space and creating an enfilade of rooms. To modernize the classical feel of the library, Kedigian chose a subtle yet vibrant blue in a high-gloss finish and a custom rug edged with a geometric Greek key pattern. **Right:** To avoid making the television the focus of the room, Kedigian hid it behind a bifold door created out of faux-leather book-bindings. **Below:** In order to keep the view open from the living room into the library, the dining room table was placed to one side and the grand piano placed in the opposite corner. A contemporary glass table surrounded by French chairs covered in Schumacher's Shockwaves further brightens and modernizes the whole look.

Q+A
with Garrow Kedigian

In a few words, describe your design style.
Streamlined classic, definitely rooted solidly in tradition, but with a modern/ contemporary twist— using pared-back detail and bolder/stronger colors and accents.

What four designers would you like to invite to dinner?
Matthew Patrick Smyth, Albert Hadley, François Catroux, and Jacques Garcia—all of whom have had a significant influence on my own personal style.

What would your perfect room look like?
A room with a lovely Palladian window and an extremely high ceiling. It would be perfectly symmetrical, with a fireplace at one end, a sofa facing the window, high-gloss walls and ceilings, and oversize plaster moldings with a dentil motif and lots and lots of Greek key!

What are some of the design rules you've had to unlearn as you've become more experienced?
Never be matchy-matchy and always trust your gut instinct. I think your first impression about any space is always the purest, and you shouldn't resist it or let it dissolve by overthinking things.

What's a design risk worth taking?
Incorporate a "foreign element" into a space, something unexpected and fabulous, something you would not normally expect to find in a room that infuses that element of edge.

Tell us ways that you've used lighting to resolve a dark room.
I always use higher gloss sheens in the paint to reflect light. I don't really love overhead lights and try to keep my use of recessed light fixtures for more utilitarian spaces such as kitchens and bathrooms. I do like to tuck floor lamps into corners of rooms, tall ones that throw ambient light and brighten up any dark corners.

How do you make your home feel welcoming?
My home is infused with a lot of color on the walls. I can't stand the sterility of white walls, and when I did my own apartments, I swore to myself that nothing would be white.

Where do you go for inspiration?
Inspiration for me can be found in anything, but mostly I try to glean inspiration from nature, colors, patterns, and textures. Color especially for me is

inspired by the late afternoon or early morning angle of sunlight.

What truly gives a home "life"?

Layering is the key to infusing life into any home. It's important to know how to mix things in different styles and colors and from different time periods—layering is the only way to make a space look like it's lived in.

Do you really need all that stuff you have in storage?

As a designer, I can appreciate things for the intrinsic value. A piece that has a history is always an inspiration to me, and I only collect and store things that I know are a valuable source of inspiration. I'm careful not to store things I know I won't ever need.

Any preferences when it comes to your bed linens?

Duvets always need to be folded neatly in thirds at the foot of the bed. I hate to see a duvet pulled across the entire surface area of a bed; it's always a lumpy and wrinkly mess.

What do you covet but can't afford?

I covet most the freedom to travel. If I didn't have my business to run, and could afford to, I think I would be in a different city every week, exploring different architecture and foods. And a private jet to help me avoid all those annoying security lines at the airports!

What's the best way to start the day?

By making my bed. I can't get started with anything else until the euro shams and decorative pillows are properly in place!

What kind of music do you listen to at home?

I always listen to classical music. I am a classically trained (amateur at that) pianist and have always enjoyed the structure of the classical repertoire. At home WQXR (New York's classical station) is always

on, and even when I am at my home in Montreal, I stream it on my Sonos system.

What smells of home to you?

Home to me is the scent of fresh-cut flowers, I always try to have them refreshed weekly. But sometimes that never happens. At holiday time, the scent of pine from a Christmas tree always signals the sanctity of home!

What's the first thing you do when you come home from a trip?

Unpack my bags and check the fridge to see if the milk is off!

What sorts of things do you still like to do the "old-fashioned way"?

I'm old school when it comes to my drawings, and I still do all my design sketches by hand. I feel like my ideas flow better onto paper with a pen in hand.

What do you hope never changes in New York?

I hope (and believe that) in New York we will always have Central Park. After a grueling day of work, it's always the best refreshment for one's head to take a stroll to clear one's thoughts. I've always lived close to the park ever since I moved to New York, and find it an essential oasis.

What small things make a bad New York day better?

A Ladurée macaron definitely makes any challenging day much better.

Is there a particular place in the city that has a special meaning for you?

My favorite spot for an early dinner (if ever I find myself in the city) on a Saturday, is to go to Freds at Barneys. When I first started my business, one of my first clients was a sweet old lady who always wanted to have our design meetings at Freds and going there always reminds me of those "good old days."

Kathryn Scott

ARTFUL AND SERENE

Above: Every detail is harmoniously arranged at Scott's Italianate brownstone. In the rear garden, a sculptural Lake Tai stone is balanced with a classically shaped urn, a koi pond, and delicate bamboo trees.
Opposite: The dining room with its grand proportions and original molding is properly furnished with Queen Anne chairs surrounding a massive table made out of a single slab of cypress.

When Kathryn Scott had to support herself after her first marriage ended, she went from being an artist to being an interior designer—not that she thinks there is a great distinction between the two. She feels that creating a harmonious living space requires much of the same skill, thought, and effort that might be poured into a work of art. Indeed, art is an essential part of our surroundings, which shape our inner landscapes.

Scott's design philosophy revolves around this idea, as well as how homes need to be places where we can replenish our creative resources depleted by the demanding world beyond—places where mundane tasks become pleasurable, and where we can connect with those we love.

Her own home, a stunning Brooklyn Heights town house, which she shares with her daughter and her husband, the well-known Chinese artist Wenda Gu, exemplifies her beliefs about the "home as sanctuary." Every object, be it an inherited antique or a piece of Asian art, seems to have space to breathe so nothing is overwhelming. There is plenty of color and yet it is not "colorful." Modern artwork is placed throughout, but doesn't dominate.

Although the architecture and scale are quite grand, particularly on the high-ceilinged parlor floor where the kitchen, dining, and living areas are situated, the rooms are peaceful and inviting. Copper saucepans hanging above the kitchen range are brightly polished and complement the dull brass kitchen fittings, and the slate side on the kitchen island serves as a chalkboard for when her daughter was at the age when she wanted to draw on walls. Generations of family china fill the cabinets, and the dining table, made from a single slab of cypress, was a gift from Scott's mother. "There's an accumulation of family history here . . . it brings in memories and associations of who you are and what you are like," Scott says.

Scott's family history has always informed her design, and this is reflected in one of her first solo projects, which remains one of her most memorable: a dacha for the president of Tatarstan. "I really loved it for a multitude of reasons: obviously the travel, but my great-grandparents were from Russia and I had this real sense of going home. The countryside looked just like the countryside around our family's summer house in Wisconsin, where my grandparents settled."

Above. In the living room, Scott's East-West approach to design is reflected in her careful placement of contrasting elements, including a delicate bamboo tree, an oversize classical statue, and a secretary that belonged to her grandmother. **Right:** A Ming dynasty opium bed is now the bed of Scott's daughter. The desk, from John Rosselli, was originally used as a coffee table.

Right: In the family kitchen and dining room, Scott was inspired by the handcrafted details she admired in the Breakers and other Newport mansions: "I wanted the space to be classic enough to be believable without re-creating a completely accurate Victorian interior." The black walnut cabinets were made on site and house three generations of family porcelain. **Below:** The painted stove hood and the copper pots hanging on iron hooks add historical references to the kitchen. The slate wall of the kitchen island is used as a chalkboard.

Left: A canopy bed, another family heirloom, stands front and center in the apricot-colored master bedroom. Inspired by old farmhouses, Scott used extra wide oak floorboards throughout the second and third floors of the house. A Navy trunk stands beneath a replica of an Albert Cheuret sconce. **Below:** In the master bathroom, a gargoyle, originally a building ornament, is now an otherworldly bathtub spout. Scott found the bathtub, sink, and fittings at Urban Archaeology. "I love the original cracks; they give the surfaces so much more dimension," she says.

Q+A
with Kathryn Scott

In a few words, describe your design style.
I find richness in simplicity. My favorite projects allow me to mix historical with contemporary, with a certain austerity in the overall feeling. Patina and texture contrasts inspire me. I prefer color to be subtle and limited, to bring out the cools and warms of the colors.

What four designers would you like to invite to dinner?
Kengo Kuma, Vincent Van Duysen, Axel Vervoordt, and Darryl Carter, though I suspect Salvador Dalí would be the life of the party.

What would your perfect room look like?
Old stone walls offset by white plaster accents, wide plank wood floors, large steel windows that open wide to the countryside, beautifully crafted hardware, high ceilings, scattered lightly with a mixture of contemporary and antique furniture, and accented by a huge ink painting by Wenda Gu.

What are some of the design rules you've had to unlearn as you've become more experienced?
1) Be careful where a client leads you with their wish list. They can unintentionally ruin the design if you take them too literally. 2) Colorful rooms often sound more beautiful than they are. 3) Trends can make a room look too predictable, which is not only boring but dates the design within a few years.

What's the simplest and best design rule?
Less really is more. Most people don't know when to stop.

What's a design risk worth taking?
Design risks are always worth taking if you believe in them. I experiment the most on myself, in case it doesn't come out quite as expected.

Tell us ways that you've used lighting to resolve a dark room.
Lighting from a variety of sources minimizes glare, and is more inviting. Lighting a wall or ceiling creates a dramatic effect and balances the light from nearby lamps.

How do you make your home feel welcoming?
Subtle colors and no clutter, with earthy materials and surfaces

Where do you go for inspiration?

Travel inspires . . . or just walk around wherever you are, taking the time to look closer at everything around you. There is plenty of inspiration right next to us.

What truly gives a home "life"?
Being with family and friends

Any preferences when it comes to your bed linens?
I love beautiful bed linens! But to me that means buttery soft percale cotton or fine linen, freshly ironed, in simple solids, with very little decorations; or antique bed linens that are hand-embroidered or home spun.

What do you covet but can't afford?
A Palladian villa in Vicenza or a seventeenth-century Dutch stone house next to a waterfall, overlooking the Hudson River

What's the best way to start the day?
Exercise, perhaps a long walk

Long hot soak in the tub or quick shower?
I love a long hot soak in a deep tub.

What job would you be terrible at?
Accounting, acting, litigating, to name a few

What kind of music do you listen to at home?
International: Tiziano Ferro, Mariza (Fado), John Lennon, Yo-Yo Ma (tango)

What smells of home for you?
Fresh-cut grass

What's your weekend routine?
I enjoy the opportunity to slow down, sleep in, spend time outside . . . going for a long walk or gardening, reading or exploring someplace new.

Do you wish you could spend more time at home?
I am fortunate to spend a lot of time at home. My office and home are in the same building. I do wish I spent more time in the countryside. I love both the city and country, but nature revitalizes me.

How long can you go without tidying up?
I always tidy up as I go; I can't relax around clutter and mess.

How do you make sure you enjoy your own parties?
Hire a caterer to prepare and serve the food and drinks

How do you subtly let guests know you want them to leave?
Start to clean the table and dishes . . . once I start to yawn, I'm reaching the end.

What sorts of things do you like to do the "old-fashioned" way?
Growing food and preparing homemade meals— direct from the garden or bought from a local farmer who believes in beyond organic.

What's the best thing about living in New York?
Everything is here. The sources of inspiration are abundant.

What's the worst thing about living in New York?
The obvious answer is too much noise, dirt, chaos, inconsideration, crowds . . . although I always wished there remained more historical buildings, as in Europe. We have a rich history, but little evidence of it, because we allowed our history to be torn down recklessly.

What do you hope never changes in New York?
Central Park

Is there a particular place in the city that has a special meaning for you?
My own home. I have lived in the same town house for thirty-three years.

Jeffrey Bilhuber

A FRESH TAKE ON LUSH ERAS

Above: An oversize mirror gives the front entry the illusion of a grander space. A curtain of simple linen hopsacking defines the area. **Opposite:** "Everything about the breakfast room is meant to coddle," says Bilhuber. A 1940s chandelier is dressed up in garnet red and gold shades. The room is wallpapered in a French nineteenth-century block print pattern by Mauny.

Jeffrey Bilhuber calls his work "a sort of wonderful burden," and makes no bones about the "Herculean" effort and energy required to be a successful interior designer. "Remember, I'm an entrepreneur. An entrepreneur's greatest fear is that without them, their business will collapse, so each day you get startled into the realization that you have to immerse yourself entirely in your job."

No one ever told Bilhuber that business and creativity could coexist within a single career. He only realized this after he made a practical decision to study hotel administration at Cornell University and, while working at the Carlyle in New York, met Mark Hampton, who had been hired to revamp some of the rooms. This meeting eventually led Bilhuber to quit his job and start looking for a new one in design. He rose quickly—one of his first clients was Hubert de Givenchy. Anna Wintour and other glittering names soon followed.

Bilhuber sees designers as barometers of change. "What makes us modern is that we're receptive. It's being responsive to the world as it changes around you." Paradoxically, a particularly powerful influence on his design is the White House of Thomas Jefferson. "It's incredible to think that he brought back pieces of furniture from Europe to influence the White House. He brought Italian architectural studies that would help him understand order, symmetry, and balance. . . . Refinement is a political ideal."

There are historical influences throughout his Upper East Side apartment. When planning his living room, he referenced New York Gilded Age interiors and the architecture of Belle Époque Paris in order to create the "muffled, peaceful world" of an Edwardian private club. A family tree hangs in the entryway; a long-lost oil portrait of an ancestor, discovered on eBay, finds space on a wall of paintings; a collection of arrowheads that once belonged to Bilhuber's grandfather is arranged on a hand-painted corner cabinet; and the walls are covered in a nineteenth-century Mauny hand-blocked wallpaper. Everything comes together to form a comforting sanctuary for both him and his young son, Christoph, who has a bright, happy room full of his Lego models and books.

Despite harking back to the past, to Bilhuber, "These rooms are modern because they're a *direct* response to the city." Ultimately, it's not about design. "It's about personality."

Above: The cosseted environment of the living room is set off by a Belle Époque suite of furniture covered in original gros point needlework and damask. The carved and gilded fillet molding captures the western light spilling into the room. **Right:** A large oil portrait of the designer's ancestor Christian Friedrich Bilhuber hangs above an emerald velvet-covered sofa. Art in gilt frames is stacked in a manner that gives the room a feeling of a grand nineteenth-century salon.

Above: Bilhuber transformed his former library into a kid-friendly space for his son, Christoph, while keeping the original brass nailheads and wall finishes. **Right:** In the master bedroom, uninterrupted panels of de Gournay wallpaper hide seven closets. A splash of gold resin by artist Nancy Lorenz adds a bolt of energy to the otherwise quiet room. "At some defining point after the install, it became clear to me that something irreverent, modern, and reactive was needed," explains Bilhuber.

Q+A

with Jeffrey Bilhuber

In a few words, describe your design style.
From the global perspective, it's how an American interprets the world that surrounds us. It's deeply personal and very biographical—I want to hear that narrative from the client. I am a very, very intuitive, creative individual.

What four designers would you like to invite to dinner?
I would not have any designers. The last thing I want to do at the end of the day is talk shop.

What's the simplest and best design rule?
Be true to yourself.

What's a design risk worth taking?
I would encourage everyone to build their confidence with color. It's about your true personality and reveals who is inside.

Tell us ways that you've used lighting to resolve a dark room.
I'm terrified of overlit rooms. I end up filling dumpsters with downlights and track lighting. Good lighting directs your attention to what's best in the room and away from what you don't want noticed.

What truly gives a home "life"?
The people who live there—the beating heart.

How do you solve your storage problems?
I don't have things in storage—I'm a user.

Any preferences when it comes to your bed linens?
Buy the best you can afford and take care of it. I'm not a wash-and-wear kind of guy. You can strike percale off the vocabulary list.

What do you covet but can't afford?
More houses! I could easily own twelve properties from Cap d'Antibes to Maine. It's the endless allure of what lies behind the garden gate. I think I really do want to be a housekeeper, polishing things, pressing linens, and waxing floors. But it's done with pride of place, not accumulation of wealth.

What job would you be terrible at?
I think I'd be damn good at almost any job. I think I'd be a very good housekeeper. I don't think I'd like to be an attendant in a vomitorium.

What kind of music do you listen to at home?
I don't. I used to, but I got past that Dirk Diggler '70s

thing of having speakers in every room. When I have guests I play scores from movies because they float through and don't pull you in. There's something I truly love about the tick of the clock in a room or the creak of a screen door, which are all about the sounds of domestic bliss.

What smells of home for you?
I have a bottle of bay rum—it's cloves—and I still put a little on in the morning. It reminds me of my father, the first smell of the morning when he gave me a kiss and then the last thing at night when he came home.

What's the first thing you do when you come home from a trip?
I am obsessed with unpacking immediately. It doesn't matter if it's 6 p.m. or 3 a.m., I can't rest until life is orderly.

Where is your favorite place to take a nap?
I had dinner with Iman, and she was saying that one day she remembers me putting my head on one end of the sofa and my feet on the other and saying, "Another victory for furniture" and falling asleep. To slump on the sofa at 2 p.m. and nap, that would be spectacular, but I don't do it often enough.

How do you make sure you enjoy your own parties?
It's all about preparation. Preplan every step of the way.

What's your favorite cocktail?
I can knock back whiskey sours with the best of them. You squeeze as many lemons as you can before you burst into tears and then a blood orange and add some simple syrup to take the edge off and bourbon. It's all about happy hour, with the emphasis on the hour—I hate going into a restaurant and being handed a menu within the first three minutes. I'm not there for the food at all—it's all about liquor and love.

What's the best thing about living in New York?
All good things come to New York.

What's the worst thing about living in New York?
I think I'm finding it increasingly noisy—it just churns on. But that's not going to change.

George, a peacock found on eBay, perpetually gazes at himself in a gilt convex mirror in Bilhuber's bedroom.

Richard Mishaan

VIBRANT ABUNDANCE

"**I'm the consummate** merchant," says Richard Mishaan, citing his entrepreneurial skills. Born in Bogotá, he lived as a boy between Columbia and the United States, an experience that, he says, taught him how to make friends easily.

He studied fine art at New York University and architecture at Columbia University, and when he graduated and found there were no jobs in New York in either discipline, he went to work for a friend in fashion on Seventh Avenue. Deciding he could go it alone in the fashion business, he later designed athleisure wear before it was a "thing." Eventually, after scoring a photo shoot with Bruce Weber and "lucking out" through various other contacts, as he humbly describes it ("I've had the luckiest career in the world"), he ended up designing high-end clothes and getting coverage in *Vogue*. He gradually moved into real estate, buying and selling property in both Manhattan and the Hamptons that, a couple of decades ago, was going for relatively cheap. That is how his interior design business started, and now, as he puts it, "We're doing it all."

His own Fifth Avenue apartment on Central Park, which he shares with his wife, Marcia Rolfe Mishaan, and their two children, Nicholas and Alexandra, is somewhat looser than his designs for clients but which very much captures the spirit of his work: powerful, vivid paintings; large, striking decorative pieces; lots of strong color; pattern on pattern. The furniture, whether antique or modern, is solidly and skillfully designed. There are plenty of animals, too, not counting his Bengal cat and two miniature Schnauzers: a giant serpent slithers in the weave of a hallway runner, the arms of a tiger-striped velvet chair take the form of carved cobras, and on coffee tables and shelves are sculptures of horses, birds, and polar bears.

Mishaan happily admits to having "more is more" taste, and although this approach is not for the faint of heart, it all works to create a home full of vitality and interest.

In the living room, a large Manolo Valdés painting and a Fernando Botero portrait hang on walls illuminated by alabaster sconces from Mishaan's former store, Homer. "Everything I've ever sold, I've wanted for myself," says Mishaan. An arrangement of Seguso crystal candlesticks and a small painting of a shell by Mishaan's wife sit on a Jules Leleu table. The custom zebra-patterned rug is from Stark.

Right: A Sherle Wagner gold-plated sink and fittings add a touch of glamour to the guest bathroom. **Below:** Front and center in the entrance hall, where there is a defiant mix of furnishing and art, a table by Guy de Rougemont displays a bold sculpture. Glass droplets by Rob Wynne hang behind *Las Meninas* by Manolo Valdés.

Above: A vibrant work on paper by Donald Baechler faces two gilt bronze chairs by Mario Bonetti that are works of art in themselves. **Right:** A Piero Fornasetti carpet depicting a slithering serpent runs the length of the hall that connects the public rooms to the private areas.

Above: A wonderfully sculptural Nuages table by Guy de Rougemont stands front and center in the library; a sofa by artist-designer Salomé de Fontainieu is positioned beneath a group of works by David Hockney, George Condo, Damien Hirst, and Fernando Botero. **Left and right:** Chairs by Garouste and Bonetti add style and comfort. Custom zebrawood bookcases are filled with art books, favorite objects, and family photographs.

Q+A
with Richard Mishaan

In a few words, describe your design style.
My design style is an oxymoron—it's classical modernism. Europeans refer to my trade as interior architecture.

Name a past designer, artist, or creative who has had the most influence on your style.
There are so many who have influenced my design sensibilities. Such modernists as Mies van der Rohe and Le Corbusier have informed the minimalist in me. Such maximalists as Renzo Mongiardino and Tony Duquette have inspired the More Is More approach I've taken in decorating. Visual artists, including Manolo Valdés, have guided me to be an artist while also being a designer.

What would your perfect room look like?
A library/media room. Mine is filled with books and art and has a media center to watch movies. It has a game table where my wife and I read, work, eat, and play games. In the end we live in that room.

What are some of the design rules you've had to unlearn as you've become more experienced?
The rule I've unlearned is that there are rules at all. Dealing with projects is like dealing with people.

Each one is different and has its own set of challenges. Some challenges are more difficult than others. Sometimes it's a collector who wants too many things in a room and sometimes it's a site condition that does not allow for something we wanted to achieve. Either way we have always worked things out and realize adversity makes us think harder and gets better results.

What's the simplest and best design rule?
If you like it, have it. Your home is where you will be spending most of your time, so don't curb your taste or wants. Mix styles if you love more than one.

What's a design risk worth taking?
Take risks with color and pattern. The more you have, the better it gets. If you get cold feet somewhere in the middle, it will not work.

Where do you go for inspiration?
History. Books on the subject. Films on the subject. Travel to historical sites in every country we visit. Museum shows. It's all there. I often say I am a designer and an anthropologist. The interesting part of design is why we live the way we live. It all comes from the past.

What truly gives a home "life"?

A sense of the occupant. Such as travel finds, items from their heritage, art work, whatever personalizes a home. We are designers who will take care of the items meant to have your life function. The perfect furniture, fabrics, wall finishes, et cetera. Then your personal items will be what people will remember and make your home come to life.

How do you design around your pets?

We are outnumbered in our home by the pets. We have three dogs and two cats. We have a dog gate that I had made in plexiglass so it would be a deterrent but not block the light or anyone's ability to see into our living room.

What smells of home for you?

The Amber candle from Homer and the Russian Nights candle by Frédéric Malle.

How long can you go without tidying up?

What? Doesn't everyone tidy up as they go along? Why let it ever get messy?

How do you make sure you enjoy your own parties?

I overplan everything. I love to have people over for dinner, so I have it down to a science at this point. The one thing I will advise everyone is that you should not micromanage after you sit for dinner, because as bad as it gets it will still be 95% perfect.

How do you stock a perfect bar?

It's interesting how tastes in liquor change over time. Summer calls for tons of rosé wine, tequila, gallons of vodka, and some red and white wine. No one drinks scotch or bourbon anymore nor do they drink gin. What you do need is good fresh-squeezed juices to make drinks with.

What's the best thing about living in New York?

You have access to everything pretty much 24/7. When you leave New York and you realize everything closes fairly early, you appreciate the city. What's even better is that you can have everything delivered to you at all hours. This does not happen many other places.

What's the worst thing about living in New York?

The worst thing is how spoiled you get being able to see the best of everything. You have the best art shows, the best performances, the best food, the best shopping, and the best people.

What small things make a bad New York day better?

A good long walk makes everything better.

Is there a particular place in the city that has a special meaning for you?

Whenever I go to Rockefeller Center and into the buildings' lobbies, the murals on the walls and ceilings are perfection. I love the skating rink, the fact that the Rockettes are in near proximity, and that there are so many shops and restaurants to visit. I also love that St. Patrick's Cathedral is across the street. I guess it's the sum of the parts that makes it seem so New York.

Lucy and Jax, the family's miniature schnauzers, lounging in their cozy beds

Tom Britt

FEARLESS GRANDEUR

Above and opposite: Gleaming blue satin upholstery on slipper chairs that once belonged to Billy Baldwin, custom sofas, crystal chandeliers, and mirrored French doors all work in concert to create Britt's aptly named Grand Salon. Oversize Chinese ginger jars, Foo dogs, and a small silver-gilt Ming table give the room a touch of the exotic.

Tom Britt's design is full of swagger, which also happens to be a favorite word of his: "Swagger to me is confidence." His aim has always been to make unforgettable rooms because he truly believes a room can make a person feel important, sexy, confident. "It's all about being unafraid," he says, "being fearless."

Britt is one of those larger-than-life designers from another era who younger peers cite as inspiration. Invariably beautifully turned out in tailored suits and with a distinctive, booming voice—which he says is still smoke-raddled from his former cigarette habit—he has a penchant for declarative one-liners about pretty much anything. On the subject of clients, "Money! You've got to have it, loud and clear!" And on design talent, "You've either got it or you don't!"

He definitely has it, and says he always did, right from when he was a young boy growing up in Kansas City, Missouri. He designed one of the rooms in his grandparents' house in an all-black scheme save for a white floor and some silver-painted screens that he made himself. He then made a fantastical garden by hanging Spanish moss, which he had stripped off trees on a visit to New Orleans, from chandeliers. Such imagination has never left Britt, which he believes is fundamental for any designer. "You can create anything out of nothing if you know how to do it."

Britt completed a degree in science from New York University before he attended Parsons School of Design. He is incredibly well read, and one of the distinctive features of his Upper East Side apartment is a full collection of Encyclopedia Britannicas bound in ivory parchment, labeled in gold, and shelved on double-faced pagoda-style bookcases inspired by the Royal Pavilion in Brighton; one could hardly imagine a building more in tune with Britt's style. And although the apartment, resplendent with electric-blue, satin-upholstered furniture and mirrored panels, could be described as opulent, it's never vulgar, always kept in check by a singular aesthetic.

Above: A narrow stairwell leading upstairs to the Grand Salon is lined with eighteenth-century neoclassical engravings. **Left:** The living room, called the Oval Room, retains its original Regency-style wood boiserie. Both the bleached wood-and-gilt chandelier and the print fabric from Brunschwig & Fils on the upholstered furniture lend the room extra flair. **Below:** The Brighton Pavilion served as inspiration when Britt designed a pair of double-faced pagoda bookcases. To blend with the colors of the room, the magazines and books were covered in white parchment paper.

Above: A small and ordinary room received a dramatic transformation by covering the walls and ceilings in their entirety with khaki-colored canvas together with a black-and-white stripe trim. Recessed wall mirrors give the room a feeling of limitless space. **Right:** In the dining room, Biedermeier chairs surround a handsome tortoiseshell table that Britt had made in Columbia. Oversize urns standing on top of statues acquired from Michael Taylor heighten the theatricality of the room.

Q+A
with Tom Britt

In a few words, describe your design style.
Classic—and of this moment

What four designers would you like to invite to dinner?
Madeleine Castaing, Georges Geffroy, Billy Baldwin, and Tony Duquette. When I was young, I studied all of these designers' creations in great depth.

What would your perfect room look like?
That answer depends on the context of the room—the geographic location, the person who lives there. Appropriateness will render perfection.

What are some of the design rules you've had to unlearn as you've become more experienced?
I've never had rules. I go into my projects with a clear vision of what each space should be. You have to have confidence. Rules inhibit creativity.

What's your best budget-friendly design hack?
Sturdy, inexpensive canvas in wonderful colors. For curtains, upholstery, slipcovers, you name it.

What's the simplest and best design rule?
I have no rules!

Tell us ways that you've used lighting to resolve a dark room.
Lighting is very important. Make sure light comes from different sources: ceiling, recessed, table lamps, floor lamps. It should come from all levels—up, down, and in the middle.

How do you make your home feel welcoming?
Make sure the lighting is right. For instance, create glamour with lighting at night. Be a good, gracious host. Make your guests feel at home and comfortable.

Where do you go for inspiration?
Travel—I've traveled all over the world. And, I've found inspiration in the rooms of certain decorators of the past—Castaing, Duquette, Geffroy, Baldwin.

What truly gives a home "life"?
Dogs are wonderful. Flowers. A fire burning in the fireplace.

How do you solve your storage problems?
I've never had a problem there.

Do you really need all that stuff you have in storage?

I used to store inventories of furniture and objects that I used for my projects. So, yes, I did need it.

Any preferences when it comes to your bed linens?
No specific preferences, as long as they're pure cotton.

How do you design around your pets?
Not a damn thing. I used to have dogs and loved them. But I did nothing to design around them.

What's the best way to start the day?
Get on the phone and start blasting away.

Long hot soak in the tub or quick shower?
Quick shower

What job would you be terrible at?
Lawyer, although my father was one

What kind of music do you listen to at home?
Cole Porter, Big Band

What smells of home for you?
Fresh flowers. For the sight and smell of them.

What's the first thing you do when you come home from a trip?
Invite people over to share my stories

How long can you go without tidying up?
I never think about it. The maid does it. That's what she's paid for. But, I am completely in charge of all arrangements—of objects, of flowers, everything.

Where is your favorite place to take a nap?
I rarely take naps.

Do you have a treasured piece of clothing in your closet?
Nothing specific. But, I love striped shirts, Charvet ties, and turtleneck sweaters in black.

How do you make sure you enjoy your own parties?
By inviting people who are lively. And, by having two friends there who I really relate to—to act as anchors.

How do you subtly let guests know you want them to leave?
I don't. They can stay as long as they want. Eileen Cecil, Rose Cumming's sister, used to call my place in Water Mill "Freedom House." People could do whatever they wanted to do. Anything goes!

How do you stock a perfect bar?
Scotch, bourbon, gin, and vodka, with vermouth and assorted mixers

What's your favorite cocktail?
When I drank, I liked Scotch. Martinis, too. Hell, I liked everything. But, I don't drink anymore.

What do you hope never changes in New York?
The theater. I love going to the theater.

What small things make a bad New York day better?
Polite and caring people

How do you get around town?
Cabs. When I was younger, I walked a lot.

Is there a particular place in the city that has a special meaning for you?
Metropolitan Museum of Art. When I was going to Parsons, I'd go there at least once a week. I particularly love the European period rooms. The Brooklyn Museum has some really good American rooms, too.

Katie Ridder

COLOR AND PATTERN

Above: In Ridder's main entrance hall, a vintage photograph hangs under a bannister that is jazzed up with a coat of scarlet paint. **Opposite:** In the living room, Julian Schnabel's *For Anna Magnani* picks up the blue, tan, and orange scheme. A pair of chairs, upholstered in Leoni fabric, sits on a room-size 1980s Agra rug from Galerie Shabab.

For Katie Ridder, a successfully designed room must contain something unexpected, an element of visual surprise. This isn't always easy to provide, but Ridder is a designer who knows exactly what she's doing even if she was never formally trained—she started out as a newbie from Northern California working for shelter magazines and "delivering laundry and whatever" at *House & Garden*. While she was there, Anna Wintour came in and changed it to *HG*. "All the editors were shortening their hems and wearing high heels," she recalls. "No one had the guts to wear sunglasses but everything changed."

Ridder eventually became a decorating editor at *House Beautiful*, where she was exposed to many different designers and had one particularly memorable experience: a well-known photographer who used a Hasselblad once encouraged her to look through the viewfinder, where the image appears upside down. This taught her to pay extra attention to how forms are arranged within a space.

Ridder's rooms are personal, practical, and colorful—truly the result of an optimistic, artistic person who wishes to provide good cheer and comfort to those who dwell in them. The extra skill that a designer brings to a project can be seen in details like the pairing of patterned lamp bases with differently patterned fabric lampshades, often in a painterly color contrast, or silver-leafing and painting the stair rail scarlet in her own Westchester home, which she shares with her architect husband, Peter Pennoyer, and their two children.

Eastern and Moorish influences, reflected in her love of Turkish Iznik tiles, add further levels of interest, although Ridder says she's increasingly drawn to old Swedish interiors. When it comes to furniture, auctions are a happy hunting ground, and her approach is characteristically straightforward: "First of all, you've got to see everything. Don't trust the catalogues, and leave absentee bids so there's no time wasted. I typically double the high estimate, and I'd say I win 75 percent of the time."

Above: A mirror from Ridder's child-hood house in California hangs above a Sheraton sofa inherited from her great-grandmother. Inexpensive silk-and-wool fabric curtains are dressed up with a hand-stenciled border. A nearby sofa is covered in a bold Greek key pattern and topped with antique textile pillows.

Right: An eighteenth-century German secretary that Ridder's husband, Peter Pennoyer, found at auction in Sweden anchors a corner of the grand living room. The lacquered Asian-style coffee table was purchased at the now-shuttered Tepper Galleries.

Right: In the dining room, red-and-white teardrop shapes inspired by the Turkish evil-eye amulets have been embroidered into the yellow backs of Regency-style chairs. A metallic wallpaper on the ceiling, grass-cloth wallpaper, and glossy moldings heighten the drama of the room. **Below:** In a windowed alcove of the library, a silk lantern designed by Ridder hangs above a sofa with seat and cushions upholstered in a boldly patterned fabric by Lulu DK. Pennoyer refinished the room's mahogany paneling himself with steel wool and linseed oil.

Above: In the master bedroom, a custom-made bed by Charles Beckley is dressed with Leontine Linens. Decorative painter Charles Hettinger painted the bedside tables in a faux-bois wood grain. **Left:** The family room is called the Zam-Zam Room for its Moroccan influences, which include a lattice screen mounted around the fireplace, leather poufs, and a brightly colored flat-weave rug purchased during a trip to Morocco. **Opposite:** Daughter Gigi's room is an effervescent combination of colors and Indian block print fabric. A pair of lacquer chests from Bungalow 5 stands on either side of a headboard covered in fabric by Lisa Fine. The striped rug is from Paul H. Lee.

Q+A
with Katie Ridder

In a few words, describe your design style.
Artistic, thoughtful, fun!

Name a past designer, artist, or creative who has had the most influence on your style.
I have always admired Renzo Mongiardino, his use of fabric combinations, and surprising contrasts in color and pattern. His designs are still fresh.

What would your perfect room look like?
Pink walls, lots of pattern with reds and pinks, lighting from many sources, and a big table to hold fresh flowers from my garden. A fireplace with a comfy chair and ottoman and an antique Oushak carpet.

What are some of the design rules you've had to unlearn as you've become more experienced?
There is nothing to unlearn, and there are definitely no rules. I've found that any mistake I've ever made has been that much more valuable in my future creativity. It's the culmination of experiences that matters most—that should be the rule.

What's your best budget-friendly design hack?
Using color on the walls is always a good place to start

What's the simplest and best design rule?
Don't overcrowd rooms. Simpler is better.

What's a design risk worth taking?
Color on the walls

Tell us ways that you've used lighting to resolve a dark room.
Uplights behind furniture, like we had in the '80s

Where do you go for inspiration?
When I can't travel, Instagram!

What truly gives a home "life"?
Fresh-cut flowers from the garden. I happen to love dahlias and peonies. And, of course, children, family, pets.

Do you really need all that stuff you have in storage?
I'm not sentimental, so everything gets given away or thrown away.

Any preferences when it comes to your bed linens?
Ideally, if one has the time, sheets are best ironed. I also happen to love Leontine Linens.

How do you design around your pets?
I think pets belong in every room. I try to design practically. Durable fabrics and nothing too precious. A good room should be designed to stand the test of time in both style and resiliency.

What's the best way to start the day?
A cappuccino!

Long hot soak in the tub or quick shower?
Tub soak!

What kind of music do you listen to at home?
I tend to have the car radio tuned to something from the 1970s.

What smells of home for you?
I adore Cathy Graham's Second Bloom candle.

What's the first thing you do when you come home from a trip?
Unpack my suitcase and water my plants.

What's your weekend routine?
Coffee, then I head to the garden and when I'm done for the day, exhausted, my husband, Peter, always has an incredible dinner waiting with wine open.

Do you wish you could spend more time at home?
I do, just to read and think.

How long can you go without tidying up?
I can't.

Where is your favorite place to take a nap?
I seldom nap, but when I'm relaxing, you can find me in the garden.

Do you have a treasured piece of clothing in your closet?
My mother's jewelry

How do you stock a perfect bar?
A little bit of everything. You never know who is going to show up!

What's your favorite cocktail?
Aperol spritz

What sorts of things do you like to do the "old-fashioned" way?
I like to needlepoint to keep busy when traveling.

What do you hope never changes in New York?
The people. I hope everyone doesn't move to Florida.

What small things make a bad New York day better?
Escaping to my favorite city garden, Wave Hill

How do you get around town?
Subway

Is there a particular place in the city that has a special meaning for you?
La Grenouille. Peter and I go there for my birthday every year.

Teddy, the family dachshund, keeping quiet watch in a corner of the stairway landing

Jamie Drake

URBANE AND WITTY

Above: In Drake's master bedroom, the dark charcoal-gray lacquer walls are a deliberate reference to the once gritty neighborhood. **Opposite:** As a contrast to the walls, Drake designed a bold crocodile-patterned headboard and coral lacquered night tables. A rug from Edward Fields based on a Van Day Truex design synthesizes the contrasting bedroom colors.

As a child, Jamie Drake remembers going to the printing plant where both his father and grandfather worked and being fascinated with the tubs of printer's ink. "I can conjure up the scent, and the colors were so *intense* and *shiny*." This experience was incredibly influential, he says, and is expressed through his own fantastic use of color.

Drake grew up in Woodbridge, Connecticut, and at the age of seven already knew he was going to be a designer. He once petitioned his "horrified" mother for a black patent-leather bedroom decorated with white trim. In his mind, that was high Hollywood chic. "I must have been a very willful child."

He went on to train at the Parsons School of Design. It was the 1970s, the black-and-white era of Joe D'Urso simplicity, and he was doing proposals with walls draped in silver-gray silk satin and polka-dot carpets in lavender, cream, and metallic gold. "I came dressed to match. I had on gold Fiorucci cowboy boots, tight cream jeans, and a purple cashmere sweater. The teachers said, 'We don't know where to look first, you or your presentation. And we don't think that's a good thing.'"

But it *is* a good thing! That same verve still informs Drake's mature work, and in his current bedroom, there is indeed a polka-dot carpet in shades of lavender, blush pink, and purple. In addition to his natural talent, Drake's experience from a career that spans more than thirty-five years shows in every inch of his grand, modern, and sophisticated space in the Chelsea neighborhood of Manhattan. Several pieces, such as the *L*-shaped sofa and the marble cocktail table, are his own design, and the bursts of color—citron, plum, and orange—are moderated by furniture upholstered in silver-grays and other neutrals. With its sixteen-foot ceilings, it's the kind of space that can take large, dramatic artwork, and Drake specifically chose it because it allows him to entertain in the way he likes: with cocktails and a buffet for large parties of up to a hundred guests.

Part of the building's allure is its much-talked-about car elevator that discreetly brings vehicles up to a private garage on each floor. "It's very cool," he admits, but what he really likes is the neighborhood. He pops into the surrounding galleries and goes out with friends every night to local bars and restaurants, even if it's a hike to Eighth Avenue. "I usually find that it perks me up, even if I'm bone-tired after a long day's work."

Opposite: Oversize soundproof windows and towering ceilings flood the apartment with light and provide unobstructed views of the Hudson River. In a living room seating area, a custom coffee table and a sectional sofa in a Donghia fabric are combined with Pedro Friedeberg's Hand chair, a low lacquered chair, and gold-leafed floor lamps by the non-profit Alpha Workshops. **Above:** Drake overcame the challenges of a structural column by enveloping it in a cabinet of ebonized wood with stainless steel and brass mesh doors. **Above right:** A colorful photograph by Thomas Ruff dominates a wall of the living room. Arranged around a custom marble and granite table are a Milo Baughman chair covered in bright orange mohair, a thirteen-foot sofa, and a pair of club chairs covered in Rubelli velvet. **Right:** An ingenious two-tier island comprises a lower gold-leaf cabinet and sweeping seventeen-foot-long Corian counter with an inlaid gold-leaf pattern across its surface, also created by Alpha Workshops. "I wanted to create a feeling of water in a river," says Drake.

A soothing lagoon-green fabric and
a mirrored wall create tranquility in
the guest bedroom, which opens up
to a private terrace. Drake designed
the leather daybed. Squares of a
Phillip Jeffries grass-cloth wallpaper
cover the walls.

Q+A

with Jamie Drake

In a few words, describe your design style.
Bold, sophisticated, urbane, and witty

Name a past designer, artist, or creative who has had the most influence on your style.
Stéphane Boudin of Jansen

What are some of the design rules you've had to unlearn as you've become more experienced?
I've learned to be less matchy-matchy and allow different metal finishes in the same room.

What's the simplest and best design rule?
Follow your gut and do what you love. Alternatively, hire a pro.

What's a design risk worth taking?
Painting your ceiling a color. Not a big expenditure (none if you're repainting anyway), and it always gives a joyous lift to a room.

Where do you go for inspiration?
Everywhere! Whether it's a block away from my apartment, or a long-distance destination such as Morocco, Denmark, Cambodia, or France, I find inspiration every day.

What truly gives a home "life"?
Objects, art, and furnishings that you love and enjoy. Especially true if they are pieces acquired on trips or that have good memories attached to them.

How do you solve your storage problems?
I am a much better editor now than I ever was. A year or so ago I had a friend with a great fashion sense spend a few hours with me. We went through my jam-packed closets piece by piece, and he told me honestly which pieces that I hadn't worn in years to get rid of. I probably donated about 60% of my clothes to charity. Cathartic!

Do you really need all that stuff you have in storage?
No, but it's almost all family things. I can't bring myself to just toss the volumes of family photo albums, et cetera. So I pay every month, and when I'm dead someone else will do the tossing.

Any preferences when it comes to your bed linens?
I indulge myself with beautiful quality custom sheets, and they get ironed.

What do you covet but can't afford?

Francis Bacon's *Three Studies of Lucian Freud*, sold to Elaine Wynne for $142 million in 2013

What kind of music do you listen to at home?
Nothing, in essence silence, when alone, or CNN (which is the antithesis of silence)

What's the first thing you do when you come home from a trip?
Take off my shoes, brush my teeth, unpack.

What's your weekend routine?
Always varies, never a routine. Depends on where I am.

Where is your favorite place to take a nap?
My bedroom. Only place I nap.

Do you have a treasured piece of clothing in your closet?
I have a thirty-year-old Gaultier peacoat with lavish gold bouillon and velvet appliqué running a third of the way up the sleeves. The nipped-waist fit is terrific, although it is sadly more roomy in the body, arms, and shoulders than current style dictates.

How do you make sure you enjoy your own parties?
Hire staff.

How do you subtly let guests know you want them to leave?
Yawn repeatedly.

How do you stock a perfect bar?
Something for everyone. So, fully stocked.

What's your favorite cocktail?
Vodka martini, up with a twist, shaken until its freezing.

What sorts of things do you like to do the "old-fashioned" way?
I prefer to read newspapers, magazines, and books in old-fashioned paper formats. I can't get used to a Kindle.

What's the best thing about living in New York?
The high-energy atmosphere. I am not a somnambulant person . . . until I'm exhausted!

What's the worst thing about living in New York?
The smell of the street corners on a sizzling hot and humid summer day. Ewwww.

What do you hope never changes in New York?
The freedom to be me, which certainly seems threatened these days nationally and globally

What small things make a bad New York day better?
Fresh bagels, manicure salons on every other corner, an abundance of bodegas with flowers for sale

Is there a particular place in the city that has a special meaning for you?
So very many. I am a sentimental person, and many buildings, vistas, streets, and benches trigger memories for me.

A sofa table displays a bronze melting clock by Salvador Dalí. The faux eyeglasses were a gift from a close friend.

John Rosselli

LIVING WITH ANTIQUES

Above: Rosselli's love for his whippets extends to collecting them in various forms. In the entrance hall, a painting of one hangs above a display of bronze whippets. **Opposite:** In his red bedroom, dog paintings surround a handsome nineteenth-century bed. A collection of porcelain whippets is grouped on the bow-fronted mahogany chest of drawers.

There is one thing that seems to hold true for antiques dealers: they are great storytellers. John Rosselli, some fifty years in the business and counting, is no exception. The husband of Bunny Williams, collector of blue-and-white porcelain, and one of the first people in the business to introduce a sophisticated mix of pieces from all over the world, he is best known for his much-loved Upper East Side decorative emporiums.

Rosselli has several showrooms around the country where he sells reproduction furniture, lighting, and fabric lines from renowned names such as Robert Kime and Raoul Textiles. At age eighty-six he renewed the lease on his antiques store on East 61st Street, and has no intention of kicking his shopping habit. "I buy something every day," he says.

He says he didn't much like school but immediately took to the antiques business, starting out as a very young man working for a pair of brothers. From them he learned to make what were basically fake antiques, presumably pretty good ones, and eventually in 1950 he set up his own tiny shop on Second Avenue and 68th Street. It was, he says, a magical time to be in the business.

His clientele has always included prominent people, including Babe Paley who bought her Christmas presents from him—he remembers selling her a little ivory palm tree that he had found in London, which she instantly deemed suitable for Truman Capote. It may all sound glamorous, but Rosselli remains humble and aware of how fortunate he is.

His childhood was spent on a prosperous farm in Newton, New Jersey, where his chores included taking out the ashes from the wood-burning stove. He grew up with six brothers and seven sisters and a large extended family; maybe this is what gives him a penchant for occasional solitude—this Upper East Side apartment is just his. He has other shared homes with his wife, including another Manhattan apartment, a country house in Connecticut, and a beach house in the Dominican Republic. But here, once or twice a week, he might just come for the afternoon to sit alone among his possessions and read. "I get myself a cup of tea, and I buy a sandwich around the corner—they make the best chicken salad and bacon sandwiches. Occasionally I have some people over for dinner." For his guests, he makes a pot roast, noodles, and a salad. "What more could you want?"

Above: A stunning nineteenth-century bamboo-and-tortoiseshell desk displays many objects. An ostrich-egg elephant container sits on a Lucite box that encases a terra-cotta camel. Against the far wall, an eighteenth-century highboy displays some of John's extensive blue-and-white porcelain collection. **Right:** The living room is filled with furniture, art, and objects collected over the years. Rosselli's particular fondness for different chair styles is evident in the space: a pair of zebra silk-velvet-covered bergère chairs is angled near a Russian chair with carved ram's-heads, and an Aubusson tapestry–covered high-back French armchair. "I've never met a chair I didn't love or covet," says Rosselli.

Left: In a corner of the living room, Portuguese silver animals are arranged with family photographs and a container made of bone.
Below: Rosselli chose mirrored walls, a formal nineteenth-century Italian chandelier, and a large mounted mirror to give the small dining room a sense of grandeur.

Opposite: Looking across an Empire daybed in the guest bedroom where the walls are filled with a collection of Orientalist paintings. "I have always loved history, and nineteenth-century paintings are so romantic, opulent, and exotic," says Rosselli. **Right:** Russian icon paintings are arranged around an Italian Directoire mirror. **Below:** Wall space in short supply, these painting and drawings find their home leaning against the guest room fireplace mantel. The wood cross on the mantel once belonged to Rosselli's mother.

Q+A
with John Rosselli

What would your perfect room look like?
There's nothing more boring than a period room. A room has to be alive with little kinky things that reveal a personality. I have a doll—it's a clown and it plays "Send in the Clowns." I've had it for forty years, and once in a while I walk in and pick it up and listen to it for a few minutes. It reminds me of a wonderful evening at the theater.

What are some of the design rules you've had to unlearn as you've become more experienced?
Surround yourself with things that you like, not things you think you ought to have.

How do you make your home feel welcoming?
If you know your guests, you know what they like. Small flower arrangements in their bedrooms are always nice, and there's always a selection of current books as well as some standard favorites. Also it's important to have a blanket that a guest can just pull over themselves if they want to take a nap. There's nothing worse than wanting to take a nap and not being able to cover yourself.

What truly gives a home "life"?
Something green, something growing.

Any preferences when it comes to your bed linens?
My wife is a bed linen connoisseur. I love the finest percale sheets, and we have antique linen that has been laundered so often that it is now very soft and very pretty. I don't like colored sheets—I like white and one big comforter. I also love Hudson's Bay blankets, which are medium-weight, woolen blankets with striped borders that were used for trade in the Hudson's Bay Company.

What do you covet but can't afford?
Oh . . . that's endless!

What have you broken that you still mourn?
I think a sense of loss comes from breaking your favorite piece of porcelain, because no matter how well it's repaired, even if it looks perfect, it's still broken.

What's the best way to start the day?
A perfect cup of tea. I'm very particular with the type and the temperature and so on. In the morning it's English Breakfast tea and in the afternoon a nice cup of Earl Grey. If I'm in the country, then I'll have smoky Lapsang souchong.

Long hot soak in the tub or quick shower?
A shower, but very long

What job would you be terrible at?
Working in a bank—anything to do with mathematics

What kind of music do you listen to at home?
I adore most Italian opera. I also love Georges Bizet's *The Pearl Fishers* and Tchaikovsky's *Eugene Onegin*. I could listen to Frank Sinatra by the hour. I knew him. He liked my Italian connections.

What smells of home for you?
Penhaligon's makes a scent called Blenheim, which I sometimes spray on dried flowers.

What's your weekend routine?
On Thursday we go to the country. We have a nineteenth-century house in a small village in Connecticut, and the first thing we do is make the rounds of the garden—the garden is very important to Bunny. There are also the dogs to look after. On Friday I make the rounds of the antiques shops—I always go on a Friday so I can get there before the weekend crowds. Twice a month we have dinner parties on Saturday nights, and I plan the menus with my wonderful assistant. We cook the meal together. We also have a wonderful gardener, who can decorate the living room by making amazing arrangements with plants that grow along the highway, things like cattails, goldenrod, and grasses—Bunny calls it "roadkill."

How do you make sure you enjoy your own parties?
Never try something you haven't tried before.

What's your favorite cocktail?
At the top of the list is a martini, because you only need a few ingredients. Most cocktails are a bore unless someone who really knows what they're doing is making them.

What sorts of things do you like to do the "old-fashioned" way?
I like a good chocolate after dinner. Is that old-fashioned?

What's the best thing about living in New York?
I wouldn't live in any other place, always exciting—sometimes for the good, sometimes not, but that's New York.

Is there a particular place in the city that has a special meaning for you?
That's a difficult one—the things I remember are no longer there!

A favorite Anglo-Indian carved camel table was purchased many years ago in London. "I think they're wonderful animals—they can be mean but they have great personalities," says Rosselli.

Scott Sanders

SLEEK LINES, BOLD COLORS

Above: Sanders's ability to work out creative solutions to design challenges is evident throughout his penthouse apartment. A pressed-wood screen slides open to the kitchen. **Opposite:** A staircase leading to the rooftop deck appears to float in the loftlike space.

Scott Sanders grew up in the small town of Piqua, Ohio, where both his father and his grandfather were builders and developers. As a boy, he went with them to pick out materials, and because he took so naturally to it, he was eventually allowed to go by himself and choose interior and exterior finishes for spec houses. "I only had one experience that ended up being an issue," Sanders recalls. "It was 1976 and I wanted to do a 'Spirit of '76' house. It was a two-story, red brick Colonial with Wedgwood blue shutters on the outside, which was fine. But the inside had red shag carpeting and Wedgwood blue cabinets with red countertops and Minutemen wallpaper. I thought it was fabulous, but no one got it."

His clients have since come around to seeing things his way, allowing him to develop his signature "New American Style." The Chelsea penthouse Sanders shares with his partner, corporate lawyer Peter Wilson, allows him to "sink his teeth" into color: a jaunty, striped Paul Smith box in the living room complements the sofa pillows, and on the dining table, a collection of jade-green, opaline 1940s French vases entices the eye. But overall, the apartment remains a "big city" pad with sleek modern lines; beneath Sanders's playfulness is keen attention to placement, scale, and function.

Sanders didn't immediately set off on the path to becoming a designer. He first studied English at Wittenberg University before working for many years as a store manager at Ralph Lauren, which is when he started studying at Parsons School of Design. Eventually, after Sanders was noticed for his ability to give design advice to customers, a position was created for him: he would become the store's first in-house interior designer. But only a week out of school, he was given the chance to design a 175-room Miami hotel.

"If I had been smarter and older, I probably would have been really scared. But I was so excited that I was like, 'Oh, sure!'"

Sanders threw himself completely into the project, even designing the china and uniforms, an approach that gave his client, the art collector Mera Rubell, some doubts. On the day of the hotel's opening, she told him, "You know, I didn't always understand what you were going for, but you were so passionate about it that I thought, 'Oh well, I'll just go with it.'" She must be glad she did—his approach was a success, and his career took off.

Left: An open floor plan in the primary living space makes the most of downtown vistas. Dark rosewood veneer on the massive fireplace surround combined with midcentury furnishings introduce a contemporary feel. Neutral gray carpeting and wall colors are punctuated with stronger colors, such as a dining room hanging light fixture of turquoise vintage glass and soft-yellow Ultrasuede upholstery on the 1960s Jens Risom swivel chairs. **Below left:** The den area features a large custom *L*-shaped sofa from Wyeth. **Below:** Open shelves display a collection of American Indian pottery and a Tramp art box. **Opposite:** In the master bedroom, *Structure IV* by Melissa Gordon hangs near a custom bed covered in fabric from Maharam. The vintage lamp is by Édouard-Wilfred Buquet.

Q+A

with Scott Sanders

In a few words, describe your design style.
Crisp and well executed, yet inherently livable

Name a past designer, artist, or creative who has had the most influence on your style.
Albert Hadley, for his extraordinary sense of order and ability to make the humble special. And Mark Hampton, for his exuberant taste. If I could be half the designer he was, it would be enough.

What would your perfect room look like?
It would be just two colors: blue and white.

What are some of the design rules you've had to unlearn as you've become more experienced?
Everything doesn't have to be blue and white. Some people actually find it boring.

What's your best budget-friendly design hack?
Inexpensive picture lights. They can make an old thrift-shop painting look like a masterpiece.

What's the simplest and best design rule?
It's not an original thought: Buy the best you can afford rather than the most of anything.

What's a design risk worth taking?

Never be afraid to use a piece that has some personal meaning attached to it, regardless of whether it's in fashion or not. Nothing can replace authenticity.

Tell us ways that you've used lighting to resolve a dark room.
Picture lights . . . everywhere . . . even on mirrors!

How do you make your home feel welcoming?
In winter in the country, it's definitely a roaring fire. In the city, it's a big bucket of ice on the bar and a bowl of potato chips. In summer, it's big bunches of flowers and plates of cookies.

What truly gives a home "life"?
Oh, come on. Love, of course! After that, laughter.

How do you solve your storage problems?
I really don't have any. I wasn't brought up to be wasteful, and I'm not a hoarder. I edit constantly. Housing Works loves me.

Do you really need all that stuff you have in storage?
The only things I won't part with are memories, so I do hang on to old photos and letters. The rest is irrelevant.

Any preferences when it comes to your bed linens?

I do like the feel of crisp, cool sheets. So anything too warm or fuzzy wouldn't be my thing. I don't know how anyone could ever sleep on flannel sheets, no matter how cold it is outside.

What job would you be terrible at?

An auctioneer or a used car salesman. I'm too soft spoken and can't sell anything I wouldn't buy myself.

What kind of music do you listen to at home?

1970s disco when I'm feeling upbeat. Adele when I'm not. And Cher all the time.

What smells of home for you?

I'm from Ohio. Apple pie.

Do you wish you could spend more time at home?

I'm really not a homebody. I love stores and restaurants so much. When I was a kid, nothing made me happier than having lunch in a department store restaurant, back when they were a big deal—something like what Bergdorf's and Barneys still have. It's the best of both worlds.

How long can you go without tidying up?

Never. I tidy constantly, perpetually. I will go to my grave plumping pillows and arranging books.

Where is your favorite place to take a nap?

Wherever our dachshund, Bailey, is

Do you have a treasured piece of clothing in your closet?

I have this thing for blue-and-white striped t-shirts. I love them. And sneakers. I guess this is how I hold on to my youth—dressing like Dennis the Menace.

What's your favorite cocktail?

I'm such a child. I like fizzy things, so right now it's an Aperol spritz. Before that became such a big deal, it was simply a glass of champagne or prosecco.

What sorts of things do you like to do the "old-fashioned" way?

I love to draw. I always have and always will.

What's the best thing about living in New York?

The energy. It's palpable everywhere.

What's the worst thing about living in New York?

The rudeness. It's an inescapable part of the culture of the city.

What do you hope never changes in New York?

Bagels and pizza

Is there a particular place in the city that has a special meaning for you?

The promenade at Lincoln Center. I remember watching Marlo Thomas strolling by all of the performance posters in the opening credits of *That Girl* and saying to myself, "I want to live there!"

In a corner of the master bedroom, a sculptural S chair by Anthony Sisto creates a nice contrast to the blue tones of the walls and carpet.

Eric Cohler

MIXING OLD WITH NEW

Above: A papier-mâché hunting trophy welcomes visitors in the front entryway.
Opposite: A painting by Wolf Kahn and an Andy Warhol Brillo box are displayed in front of a bookcase filled with art and design books.

Eric Cohler says his paternal grandmother had the best taste of anyone he ever met, and considers himself blessed to have grown up in a New York family that has a history of collecting both contemporary art and "fantastic" antique furniture. "Some people could have been turned off by it; I actually embraced it," Cohler says.

His work reflects this: mixing old with new, expensive with inexpensive. He prefers to spend money on art rather than on furniture, and often uses paint for an architectural effect because he believes saturated colors make a room seem larger than it actually is. His starting point for a room is frequently fabric, perhaps a rug, and he then radiates outward from that one central idea, like the spokes of a wheel.

Despite being dyslexic, he is a voracious reader, and says books are "like oxygen and water" for him; he keeps his collection of over ten thousand volumes in a warehouse in Queens. He is as much an academic as an interior designer, graduating with two degrees from Columbia University, one in art history and English, and one in historic preservation. He went on to study architectural design at Harvard, and is now an adjunct professor at Hobart and William Smith Colleges. While at Columbia, he started taking on small jobs from his mother's friends to pay his student expenses and hung out his shingle there and then. He's been on his own ever since.

Perhaps it helped to have a mother who was also an interior designer—that is until she decided to join his father's profession and become a psychoanalyst. Cohler considered being a psychoanalyst "for two seconds," but points out how he does something similar when it comes to listening closely to his clients.

A self-described "Bedouin," Cohler has lived in more than twenty apartments since college and relishes the chance to reinvent rooms. In fact, he enjoys change so much that he thinks most interiors should be reevaluated every five to ten years. Interestingly, despite all this change, and for someone with such restless energy and flair, his aim is to make rooms feel like places of security, including those in his Beekman neighborhood apartment. "I want to feel enveloped and cosseted. To feel not only secure in my own space but also surrounded by wonderful things. To me, that's the ultimate luxury."

Left: In the living room, Cohler cleverly found more space for his burgeoning art collections by hanging pieces in front of the apartment windows. A small standing mobile by Alexander Calder and a work by Roy Lichtenstein are arranged on a lacquer table from Antony Todd. **Above:** In the den, a deep charcoal paint color serves as a dramatic backdrop for the art collection. A painting by David Salle hangs above a plush olive-green velvet sofa. A Caucasian rug, abstract animal-print pillows, and an ikat-covered French chair add further layers of pattern. **Right:** Griffin and Olivia, Cohler's standard poodle puppies, pose for the camera. Nearby, a Roman statue is contrasted against an abstract painting purchased at auction.

Right: In the master bedroom, a portrait by Alan Katz of the artist's wife hangs above a custom tufted headboard. Pop art prints by Andy Warhol, *Marilyn Monroe* and *Flowers*, are mixed with traditional English mahogany furniture. **Below:** A painting commissioned by Cohler—which incorporates copied sections of works by American artists Edward Hopper and John Singer Sargent—hangs in a corner of the master bedroom.

Q+A

with Eric Cohler

In a few words, describe your design style.
I'm a trained classicist with a veneer of modernity.
I understand the basic tenets of architecture and
design and therefore know when to break the rules
and when not to play with perfection.

**What four designers would you like to invite
to dinner?**
It would be a mix of those living and those on
the other side: David Hicks, Billy Baldwin, Nicky
Haslam, and Jennifer Post. The "designer" who has
influenced me most is a style maker in the grand
tradition—my paternal grandmother.

What would your perfect room look like?
Anne Bass's living room designed by Mark Hampton—
I was there for a cocktail party and didn't want to
leave. It's a timeless mix of Abstract Expressionist
works of art including huge Mark Rothko canvases
and Georgian furniture covered in an off-white linen
damask; and the sweeping views of Central Park are
the kicker.

What's your best budget-friendly design hack?
Here's my trick. I cut out black and white vintage
photos from books and have them framed beautifully.

It's a lot of look for the cost of a frame. Make sure to
use a large mat

What's the simplest and best design rule?
The best design rule I recommend is to edit, edit, edit.

What's a design risk worth taking?
Color is the easiest way to make the largest impact.
Walls can always be repainted if you hate it.

**Tell us ways that you've used lighting to resolve a
dark room.**
Lighting can make or break a space. LED bulbs
are a saving grace as they light up even the darkest
corners. I prefer the 2700 bulb because it's less harsh
and closer to ambient.

How do you make your home feel welcoming?
Good lighting, comfortable furniture, great art,
excellent food, drink, family, and friends

How do you solve your storage problems?
By creating walk-in closets even if it means making
rooms slightly smaller.

**Any preferences when it comes to your
bed linens?**

I usually like them white and crisp. I make my bed with military precision daily (or at least try to).

How do you design around your pets?
Designing around pets is always challenging. The key is not to let the pets rule the roost. Create a stylish yet comfortable environment for both you and the pets, where you won't worry when your dog jumps on the sofa.

What do you covet but can't afford?
An early 1960s Mark Rothko color field painting. Throw in a John Singer Sargent swagger portrait and an Edward Hopper New York scene for good measure.

What's the best way to start the day?
I start the day with a song as soon as I hit the shower, usually something by Rodgers and Hammerstein.

What job would you be terrible at?
I'm utterly hopeless at anything having to do with math.

What kind of music do you listen to at home?
Jazz, Sinatra, Miss Billie Holiday, and anything by Handel

What smells of home for you?
Fresh linens

What's the first thing you do when you come home from a trip?
I always straighten the pictures (scout's honor!) and then unpack.

What's your weekend routine?
I try to get out of the city to my family place in northern Connecticut, as many weekends as possible. It's nine acres of meadow and belonged to Dorothy and Richard Rodgers. The hills are definitely alive!

How long can you go without tidying up?
I last about ten minutes before my OCD kicks in.

Do you have a treasured piece of clothing in your closet?
My favorite piece of clothing is a navy blue Hermès cashmere polo coat that I bought at an outlet sale for $500 twelve years ago. It still looks like new.

How do you make sure you enjoy your own parties?
I hire help to serve and tend bar, otherwise I'd have to ask the guests, "How was my party?"

How do you stock a perfect bar?
I stock my bar with the basic crowd pleasers plus a few surprises from my travels—a vintage Asprey cocktail shaker, a Jensen cactus-pattern bottle opener, French art moderne linen cocktail napkins, my parents' Danish modern ice bucket circa 1956, and my great-grandmother's Venetian glass condiment containers.

What's your favorite cocktail?
A Bramble. Scott's in London mixes the tastiest one as far as I'm concerned.

What sorts of things do you like to do the "old-fashioned" way?
For me there's no replacement for a pen and paper even though my handwriting is illegible. Ditto for a book and music recorded on vinyl.

How do you get around town?
I walk, take the subway, taxi, or Uber.

What's the best thing about living in New York?
Aside from the raw energy and accessibility to the best of the best, it's how easy it is to escape town when that energy becomes cacophonous.

What's the worst thing about living in New York?
The summer humidity, smells, and crowds

What do you hope never changes in New York?
I hope that the ever-expanding New York skyline always allows a visual void to see the sky.

Robert Couturier

PARISIAN BOHEMIAN

Above: In the library, eighteenth-century Danish chairs stand next to a cabinet by Alfred Porteneuve that was made for Couturier's grandfather's office in Paris.
Opposite: In the living room, an enormous photograph of a flower by Ron Agam hangs above a white sofa decorated with mismatched pillows. On the floor is an oversize nineteenth-century Persian rug.

Robert Couturier was raised by his Parisian grandmother in what he calls a "glam house" in the 16th arrondissement; its interiors were designed by Jean-Michel Frank. He also spent time in various vacation homes including one in the mountains that had been designed by a British gentleman in a "very, very, very elegant" 1920s style. It's therefore not surprising that his own taste has been shaped by a lifetime of exposure to beautiful things.

Couturier regards his country house in Kent, Connecticut, as his true home, but his SoHo apartment is home for the working week. It has high ceilings and a Parisian bohemian feel thanks to several perfect juxtapositions. These include a brilliantly colored rug from Turkestan that sets off a zebra-striped sofa and a pair of huge Flemish-style octagonal mirrors. Each morning, his bed is made up with various pillows and an exquisite Jean-François Lesage hand-embroidered cover, transforming it into a sumptuous divan for daytime use. A simple, sculptural bronze ladder provides access to storage space. There are quite a few proper pieces in the apartment, such as an important Louis XVI commode and a Jacques Adnet leather desk and chair, but a large orange exercise ball and other exercise contraptions are equally visible.

Couturier is not someone who takes himself too seriously. He's a fan of the *Real Housewives* series and a fiend for sugar, especially macarons from Payard. He doesn't hesitate to admit to making design mistakes, such as the time a chandelier collapsed on a dining room table, and he likes to speak his mind: "Suburban developments should be banned. They buy these giant houses with these giant kitchens and family rooms that look like cathedrals." And although he admires well-executed minimalism, he finds this style ultimately unforgiving, unlike rooms full of color and pattern, which, he says, can take more of a beating.

He is genuinely unfussed when the dogs sit on a little armchair that once belonged to Marie Antoinette. Indeed, his five beloved dogs can do pretty much whatever they like. Dogs and people—they are all that really count. "Things are of no importance to me; I like to look at them, but things come and go. I now finally have all the beautiful things I was brought up with, but there is nothing I cannot part with."

Right: A billowing plaster screen and a large photograph by Michael Eastman are positioned in front of a light wood wall that doubles as additional storage space in the living room. **Below and below right:** A long oak table by Maurice Savin and Jaques Adnet stands in front of a pair of sconces by Armand-Albert Rateau. Another Ron Agam photograph hangs over the sofa. Exquisite hand-beaded silk fabric from Combray covers the back of a French chair, and a nineteenth-century Persian carpet is layered on top of a white rug.

Right: The bedroom space also serves as Couturier's home office. In the sitting area, ebony-and-tortoise mirrors flank a portrait by Richard Cosway. The cabinets are nineteenth-century English. **Below:** A pair of 1930s French armchairs are both chic and comfortable. On the far wall, a photograph by Gerald Incandela hangs above a cabinet by Alfred Porteneuve.

Right: A 1940s daybed topped with an ornately embroidered gold pillow is tucked behind a curved wall. **Below:** Couturier's desk is placed between two curved walls that conceal dressing and sleeping spaces. Photographic portraits by David Seidner hang on either side of the designer's desk area.

Opposite: An elegant dressing space is tucked into a corner of the office behind a curved wall. A silk-covered French chair is positioned next to a French black-and-red lacquered table displaying favorite objects and snapshots. The photograph is by Israeli artist Nir Arieli.

Q+A
with Robert Couturier

In a few words, describe your design style.
I really don't have a style! And I am not joking when I say that what I like is to make people happy and in order to do that I have to give them the house they want, not the one that I would want or would like for myself. There are things that I prefer and styles that I find more comfortable living with, but I would not want to impose my tastes on others!

What four designers would you like to invite to dinner?
Henri Samuel, Stéphane Boudin, Brian McCarthy, and Stephen Sills. We would have a great conversation!

What would your perfect room look like?
I would be terminally happy at the Petit Trianon. There is nowhere else that I find more beautiful!

What are some of the design rules you've had to unlearn as you've become more experienced?
Absolutely unlearn what you think is good taste or taste in general!

What's your best budget-friendly design hack?
Not sure what the question means, but I suppose a clever way to save? I would be the worst counsel for that, because I have a bad tendency to look at prices after I have bought something . . .

What's the simplest and best design rule?
Understand the clients for who they are and not what you want them to be! And apply yourself to making them happy!

What's a design risk worth taking?
Mixing strange colors together!

Tell us ways that you've used lighting to resolve a dark room.
Multiple sources of lighting. The more the better. And all dimmable!

How do you make your home feel welcoming?
You don't really make your *home* feel welcoming; *you* are a welcoming person! It does not matter how many fresh flowers you have or how pretty your home is. If you are not welcoming, it will still be deadly!

Where do you go for inspiration?
Everywhere . . . you find it in everything.

How do you solve your storage problems?

Send everything to auction once in a while, and throw out what has been on your desk and that you don't remember what it is. As far as clothes, I hang them under white cloth in the attic. I cannot throw out clothes.

How do you design around your pets?
I don't. They live where I live, sleep where I sleep, and sit where I sit!

What have you broken that you still mourn?
There is nothing material that I have broken that I mourn! AT ALL. I mourn very many broken relationships though and so many beloved pets. Easy to replace stuff, difficult to replace people and dogs.

What kind of music do you listen to at home?
Classical music, specifically baroque and mostly Bach

What smells of home for you?
Frédéric Malle's Cafe Society scent, because it is the way our houses smelled when we were kids, a combination of Guerlain house perfume, ashes, and a bit of humidity

What's the first thing you do when you come home from a trip?
Unpack! After I have played with the dogs and said hello to my husband.

How long can you go without tidying up?
Three minutes! I have my linen bed sheets ironed everyday! There is nothing I hate more than a mess, especially a dirty one.

How do you make sure you enjoy your own parties?
As a friend of mine said, only have people to your house whom you like or whom you are curious to know. And always have an excellent cook, nothing worse than bad food! If you are bored AND have bad food then there is no good issue . . .

How do you subtly let guests know you want them to leave?
I don't. I think it is rude. They are my guests, and if they stay it means they are having a good time. Plus, I only have friends over so I am thrilled when they are with me. If it really is getting too late I say that I have to let the dogs out, which is always true!

What sorts of things do you like to do the "old-fashioned" way?
Being polite, courteous, and elegant

What's the best thing about living in New York?
There are so many best things . . . The Met Opera, the Met museums, all my friends, MoMA, Carnegie Hall. So many things. But above and beyond, it is the home I chose for myself, not the one imposed by circumstances.

What's the worst thing about living in New York?
The increasing filth, the incessant traffic, and people walking like zombies, their eyes on their iPhones. But that is everywhere!

What do you hope never changes in New York?
I hope New York keeps changing all the time—that is what makes this city interesting and different from most others. If I had to choose something, I'd say keep Majorelle, the restaurant Charles Masson has opened. I could have every meal there!

How do you get around town?
I used to have a car and a driver, then I realized that they were costing me a large mortgage. Now I go around with Uber!

Is there a particular place in the city that has a special meaning for you?
The Frick Museum, which does feel like home to me. It is the place I go to, or the Wrightsmans Galleries at the Met, when I have a bad case of the blues.

Brian Sawyer

SURROUNDED BY CHERISHED OBJECTS

Above and opposite: The paneled foyer, which functions as a gallery and dining room, is painted in Benjamin Moore's Witching Hour blue and displays a notable collection of taxidermy, much of it inherited from Sawyer's granduncle.

"I just can't deny myself a beautiful thing," admits Brian Sawyer, whose Greenwich Village apartment is filled with a delicate arrangement of the exquisite, the intriguing, and even the slightly strange. Taxidermied swifts and swallows in midflight hang from a wall, and beneath them a snowy owl glares from its perch on a glass display case that houses an elegant stuffed swan surrounded by meadow rushes. There are Thracian jars from Bulgaria, ammonites and amulets, ostrich feather dusters, a bas-relief of Oscar Wilde, a couple of contorted Chinese scholar's rocks, and, in the drawers of cabinets, seashells, hunks of jade, and unopened packets of old letters on onionskin paper.

Despite all these oddities, the word *eccentric* doesn't quite come to mind. The slate and silver grays of the walls are too artfully chosen and act as perfect backdrops for the displays, and the antique furniture is deliberately contrasted with good modern pieces, all placed with an educated eye. And because everything is so authentic, the apartment doesn't have a trendy "retro" vibe; there is a genuine bit of history contained here.

As a child growing up in Indianapolis, Sawyer loved to amass and arrange collections of seashells, crystals, and geodes. His plant collection eventually became so big that his parents had a greenhouse built for it.

Sawyer descends from farmers who originally emigrated from Holland in the 1870s, and although he is a partner in the multidisciplinary, high-end architecture firm Sawyer Berson, he doesn't consider himself to have fallen so far from the tree. His first love is landscape design, which he studied at the University of Virginia, and his first job was with the Central Park Conservancy. He eventually moved on to work for Robert A.M. Stern Architects, where he became the head of landscape architecture.

Although his day-to-day design primarily involves working on large, impressive residences both inside and out, Sawyer still has a modest dream yet to be realized: he wants to design the garden he once tried to create as a child. "It's a lawn full of clover and violets, surrounded by a bed of nicotiana, the white flowering tobacco—they're star-shaped and they open mostly at night. Under a full moon, the garden looks like it has millions of white butterflies in it."

Left: Looking across the carefully layered dining room table into the living room, the Maison Jansen–inspired table with a cordovan leather top is by cabinetmaker Gregory Gurfein, and the chairs are by Kaare Klint.
Below left: The living room has a large skylight that illuminates more of Sawyer's art and collections, which include scholar's rocks. **Below:** A sculptural bronze repoussé panel and a photograph of a Greek head by Fernando Bengoechea hang above an earth-tone sofa and chunky coffee table. **Opposite:** Guest bedroom walls are covered in brown Ultrasuede. "Not my usual choice but it goes well with the speckled olive marble fireplace mantel," says Sawyer. A 1960s leather chair stands near an antique Chinese table displaying more treasures.

Q+A
with Brian Sawyer

In a few words, describe your design style.
Eclectic and traditional

What would your perfect room look like?
The perfect room would be traditional or modern but always with proportions using the golden mean and with windows on three sides.

What are some of the design rules you've had to unlearn as you've become more experienced?
Setting any rules will eventually work against you.

What's your best budget-friendly design hack?
Make a cheap artwork look expensive with a fancy frame.

What's the simplest and best design rule?
"Keep it simple, stupid!"

What's a design risk worth taking?
Anything you've never done before

Tell us ways that you've used lighting to resolve a dark room.
Resign yourself to the darkness and make it beautiful: Use deeper, richer colors, softer finishes, and less lighting than you think is necessary.

How do you make your home feel welcoming?
Make sure there is always plenty of delicious food and drink at the ready.

Where do you go for inspiration?
Almost anywhere, as long as I've never been there before.

What truly gives a home "life"?
You can decorate ad nauseam, but it really comes down to the people who inhabit a space and the layers of memories.

How do you solve your storage problems?
I don't. I just get more storage.

Do you really need all that stuff you have in storage?
"Need" is quite beside the point; it's about knowing that it's there.

How do you design around your pets?
I lost that battle long ago. She does whatever she pleases.

What do you covet but can't afford?
A 1970 metallic dove-gray Mercedes 600D with

butterscotch interiors and a chauffeur to drive it

What have you broken that you still mourn?
A delicate and exquisite nineteenth-century plaster bas-relief of a human skull that I found in the flea market in Milan

What's the best way to start the day?
French Market coffee and the print version of the *New York Times*

Long hot soak in the tub or quick shower?
Quick shower

What kind of music do you listen to at home?
Classical solo piano

What smells of home for you?
The mushroom-y sootiness of a well-used fireplace

What's the first thing you do when you come home from a trip?
I open all the windows.

What's your weekend routine?
There's no actual routine. I try to garden as much as possible in the summer and ski as frequently as I can in the winter in addition to catching up with friends.

Do you wish you could spend more time at home?
Yes, but whenever I actually do, I can't wait to get out.

How long can you go without tidying up?
Twenty-four hours

Where is your favorite place to take a nap?
The green velvet chair under the skylight in the living room

Do you have a treasured piece of clothing in your closet?
A collection of Romeo Gigli suits from the early 1990s

How do you subtly let guests know you want them to leave?
A sudden pronouncement, "It's time to walk the dog."

How do you stock a perfect bar?
Sparkling glassware, perfect ice cubes, and more booze than a small party could drink in one night

What's your favorite cocktail?
In the summer: mezcal margarita. In the winter: a Rob Roy "perfect"

What sorts of things do you like to do the "old-fashioned" way?
Handwritten thank-you notes with antique stamps

What's the best thing about living in New York?
It's the energy of the people—the consistent influx of energy that keeps you moving forward whether you like it or not.

What's the worst thing about living in New York?
Chain stores

What do you hope never changes in New York?
That young people want to move here

What small things make a bad New York day better?
Unsolicited kindness. A kind gesture to or from a stranger.

How do you get around town?
I walk wherever I can, and take the subway where I can't.

Is there a particular place in the city that has a special meaning for you?
The Conservancy Garden in Central Park. At my first job in the city at the Central Park Conservancy the windows in my office looked onto it.

Anthony Baratta

DESIGN WITH HAPPINESS IN MIND

Anthony Baratta's Chelsea apartment remains true to the bold and exuberant style he has consistently showcased over his thirty-year-and-counting career. Deploying a strong palette of rich browns, black, taupe, and dark yellow tones, in addition to geometric patterns, Baratta combines zebra, leopard, and giraffe print fabrics on oversize chairs and sofas with sleek Danish modern pieces. He refers to his African-inspired accent stools as "Belgian Congo Deco" and sets them alongside his real Art Deco side tables.

And then there are "the men"—everywhere. The eye is immediately drawn to the classical sculptures, photographs, drawings, and other images of beautiful, muscular, and mostly naked figures that decorate every room in Baratta's apartment. These include a set of hanging Fornasetti plates, which together form a collage of the biblical Adam, and a marquetry image of Arnold Schwarzenegger carved into the back of a cheval mirror bought at a New Orleans auction. Baratta's apartment represents his wit and sheer skill, which allow him to pull off such a unique look while retaining a feeling of sophistication and control. He sees himself as "quintessentially all-American," and loves to incorporate quilting, appliqué, needlepoint, and cabinetry into his work. These folk crafts have "an old-world elegance," he says.

Baratta states that he always looks for the fun in what's new. Fun was very much ingrained in the vividly colorful aesthetic he created with his late business partner, William Diamond, in their design firm, Diamond Baratta. They once posed on a pair of thrones upholstered in giraffe print for their website and referred to themselves, tongue in cheek, as geniuses. Now forging ahead with only his name on the shingle, Baratta still thinks of Diamond every day. "Both Bill and I had a hard time doing very, very traditional decorating."

In the master bedroom, Baratta combined two Victorian sofas to create a fabulous bed for himself. He angled the bed on a custom geometric-patterned carpet and placed a low "Belgian Congo Deco" style table within reach for bedtime reading. Nearby, he rested a humorous "portrait of an ugly man" on a black-and-white easel from London.

Above: The living room is defined by strong combinations of textures and patterns in a variety of neutral tones. Art Deco–style chairs in a jazzed-up herringbone check are placed opposite a curvaceous leopard-patterned sofa and a boomerang gray-and-white terrazzo table. **Above right:** A small Memphis side table, which once belonged to legendary fashion designer Geoffrey Beene, stands on a custom rug made out of coat fabric. **Right:** Classical sculptures, including an oversize plaster cast of a Roman man, populate much of the apartment. Baratta's father once asked him if he couldn't put underwear on some of them.

Above: Baratta's preference for the lines of curved furnishings, no matter what period, is clear in his choice of a tufted Victorian sofa and a treasured Tulip Chair by Erwine and Estelle Laverne. A Harlequin lamp stands next to a Danish Modern chair picked up at a local thrift shop.
Right: Stainless-steel shelving by USM is filled with a mix of classical sculpture, framed photographs, and art books.

Baratta meticulously designed this massive neoclassical cabinet to hide the living room television as well as to provide extra storage space. Another statue of a Roman man stands nearby. "I have a big living room just to hold all these men," Baratta says.

Q+A
with Anthony Baratta

In a few words, describe your design style.
My designs are quite varied in style, but they all have lots of color, pattern, and exaggerated scale—and a bit of whimsy. I design with happiness in mind.

What four designers would you like to invite to dinner?
Michelangelo, Ward Bennett, Robert Adam, and Thomas Jefferson

Name a past designer, artist, or creative who has had the most influence on your style.
Without a doubt, I am most influenced by Matisse.

What would your perfect room look like?
My perfect room would have a wall of glass looking out to a beautiful view. It would be colorful and cluttered with all my stuff and would have fresh flowers all the time.

What's the simplest and best design rule?
Stay away from trendy decorating. Design is like fashion. It goes out of style really quickly. Never use a sectional sofa.

What are some of the design rules you've had to unlearn as you've become more experienced?

I've learned that, as Woody Allen wrote in the movie *Interiors*, "Decorating is not an exact science." Contrived rooms are dead to me. Don't overplan.

What's your best budget-friendly design hack?
Paint your tired old floors.

What's a design risk worth taking?
Never be afraid of color. I simply don't know how to do beige interiors.

Tell us ways that you've used lighting to resolve a dark room.
Honestly, nothing tricky. Lots of interesting, dimmable lamps. I never use those stupid light bulbs of today.

Where do you go for inspiration?
Art and travel

What truly gives a home "life"?
Books and more books. They reveal your personality.

How do you solve your storage problems?
Oh my! I have so much storage! It is a constant and expensive problem.

What's the best way to start the day?
Meditation then the treadmill or a walk

What kind of music do you listen to at home?
Electronic dance music and classic disco

What smells of home for you?
My Adrift candle from my shop. No kidding, it was designed for me.

What's the first thing you do when you come home from a trip?
Schedule a massage. Take my clothes to the cleaners.

Do you wish you could spend more time at home?
Not really. I spend too much time at home already.

How long can you go without tidying up?
About five minutes. I teach all my young designers that they must keep their homes clean and well organized if they are asking for clients to do the same.

Where is your favorite place to take a nap?
I guess my favorite place is on my living room sofa. It's been in cheetah silk velvet forever, and it's so comfy.

Do you have a treasured piece of clothing in your closet?
I have the most gorgeous jacket from the Tom Ford era at Gucci. It's pieced velvet in a David Hicks pattern. Beyond beautiful.

How do you make sure you enjoy your own parties?
I try to do my best to make as many introductions as I can. I don't enjoy a party if people feel left out.

What sorts of things do you like to do the "old-fashioned" way?
Draw. I don't know how to draw on the computer, and wouldn't enjoy it if I did. Drawing is the soul and the language of design.

What's the best thing about living in New York?
All-night delis and diners

What's the worst thing about living in New York?
Having to go to any emergency room at any hospital in NYC

What do you hope never changes in New York?
The Rose Main Reading Room at the New York Public Library

How do you get around town?
By subway or taxi. I hate Uber.

Is there a particular place in the city that has a special meaning for you?
The Metropolitan Museum of Art. I worked there for all my college years. I still feel a sense of wonder there.

In the master bedroom, a marquetry rendition of Arnold Schwarzenegger covers the back of a cheval mirror purchased at auction in New Orleans.

Deborah French

SOULFUL ECLECTICISM

Above: A gate from India divides the living room from the dining area.
Opposite: The living room is filled with items that reflect French's love of Morocco and Asia. A coffee table made from a nineteenth-century grain grinder from India stands in front of a low *U*-shaped sofa covered with a mix of suzani pillows. *Prayer*, a photograph by Ron Hamad, is flanked by a pair of wrought-iron lanterns.

When Deborah French was going around with her portfolio looking for a job, the director of Ralph Lauren Home saw the photographs of the stunning stone house in Mykonos that she designed and said, "Oh, I know this house. We've used it on inspiration boards for Ralph." Needless to say, she got the job as director of store development and worked there for over six years designing stores all over the world, including the largest flagship, the Omotesando shop in Tokyo.

That portfolio wasn't the only one she was schlepping. French had also worked as a sittings editor for the formidable fashion editor Polly Mellen prior to moving to Greece with her then-husband, and had one for fashion and one for her sculpture. At heart, she remains a sculptor—her skills in that medium are evident in the soft, organic shapes featured in the much-published Greek stone house.

The career shift to interior design was, she says, quite a challenge. "I had never even written out a purchase order." But besides Ralph Lauren, her "original spirit" caught the eye of other prestigious employers such as hotelier and entrepreneur Ian Schrager.

And that originality is definitely what you get in her design. In her Tribeca loft, rich mixes of fabrics are key. Flat-weave kilims are contrasted with higher-end velvets, and a delicate Scalamandré print on a chaise longue in the bedroom complements a suzani-covered headboard. The burnt orange in both fabrics is brought out by two large pillows on the bed in the same color. Pretty much everything in the loft comes from somewhere exotic: Nubian baskets were brought back from a family trip to Egypt in the 1970s, and a coffee table was once a nineteenth-century grain grinder in India. French's own intriguing sculptures—life-size clay and metal studies of women—exemplify the spirit sought by other tastemakers.

The fact that people desire what she has to give still seems to surprise her. "I look at myself and say, 'Gee, if I had just stayed in one straight line, I would have had a career!'"

Left: Several seating areas make casual entertaining easy in the open loft space. A small wooden bride's chair from Afghanistan and scattered kilim-covered pillows are strategically placed for lounging. **Below left:** An antique wood-and-iron coffee table from Morocco stands in front of a Ralph Lauren sofa. **Below:** French's son, Ilias, has a room that reflects a cheerful mix of influences, with a zebra-covered African drum table, kuba cloth pillows, and a guitar mounted beneath an oversize wall clock. **Opposite:** A late-nineteenth-century Italian chandelier hangs above a custom dining table. French chairs are covered in a mustard-colored linen.

Opposite: In the kitchen alcove, the designer hung a copy of a Fernando Botero painting above a Swedish bench. Antique French garden chairs surround a Moroccan tile table. **Right:** In French's bedroom, suzani fabric is used for a bold headboard, and what looks like a religious painting is in fact a seventeenth-century wooden church shutter. **Below:** Light enters the room through the frosted glass panels of the refurbished casement that French used to divide the bedrooms from the open living spaces. She often sources architectural salvage from the Demolition Depot.

Q+A
with Deborah French

In a few words, describe your design style.
"Eclectic" is the general style term from the usual list of choices. I use a lot of color, texture, and variety with pieces from different parts of the world and various time periods to create an elegant yet very warm and welcoming atmosphere, mixing both high and low elements together. I believe a home should feel as if it has a soul.

What four designers would you like to invite to dinner?
As long as this is a fantasy I'll invite a mix of people, living and deceased, for a wonderful, home-cooked dinner. Richard Hare, a once notable New York interior designer, who decorated the house I grew up in. It certainly had a big influence on me. Eileen Gray, because I would love to tell her how much I adore the interiors she designed, which were so far ahead of their time and are still so modern looking. Roberto Baciocchi, because I adore his house in Arezzo, Tuscany. What he did with color and texture is superb. And, any one of the great fifteenth-century painters of Siena, because their color palette is so extraordinary and has had a great influence on my own use of color.

What would your perfect room look like?

It would have a lot of sunlight and a beautiful view, and be cozy and relaxed. It doesn't need to be perfect.

What are some of the design rules you've had to unlearn as you've become more experienced?
I was trained as a sculptor so I've worked very intuitively as a designer. There has been a lot to learn over the years but nothing I can think of to unlearn yet.

What's the simplest and best design rule?
Believe in what you're doing and put your heart into it.

What's a design risk worth taking?
Using color

What do you covet but can't afford?
I would love to have homes in several places in the world and a boat to travel the entire Mediterranean, with none of the headaches that go along with them!

What have you broken that you still mourn?
Not a thing! That would just be a waste of time, and I'm so grateful for my life.

What's the best way to start the day?

Yoga and/or stretching followed by meditation

What job would you be terrible at?
Acting

What kind of music do you listen to at home?
That depends on my mood. Lately, I'm loving Philip Glass's piano solos. They allow me to think and are very soothing.

What's your weekend routine?
I don't have routines. I love variety!

What's your favorite cocktail?
Death's Door gin, fresh lime juice, raw organic agave, and ice

What sorts of things do you like to do the "old-fashioned" way?
I like to cook and bake the "old-fashioned" way rather than order in or get ready-made dishes.

What's the best thing about living in New York?
For me, my home, family, and friends are the best thing about being in New York, yet the reason we're all here is for the fabulous culture, food, diversity, and the vast opportunities to fulfill ourselves personally and professionally.

What's the worst thing about living in New York?
For me, the weather in winter and the increased noise are the worst things about being here.

What do you hope never changes in New York?
Diversity and creativity, as well as the human scale of some of the neighborhoods

What small things make a bad New York day better?
Sunshine and smiles from strangers

How do you get around town?
I mostly use the subway, because I have the major lines all converging around City Hall within a couple of blocks of me—otherwise, coming from Tribeca to many parts of the city would take time in a taxi or car service. Actually, I live in subway heaven!

Is there a particular place in the city that has a special meaning for you?
I love The Odeon, in Tribeca. Before it was The Odeon it was Towers Cafeteria, and I would go there sometimes for breakfast. You could get two eggs, a bagel, and coffee for 97 cents! The Odeon replaced it in 1980, and to this day I never tire of going there. It's a classic!

Simba, relaxing in the bathtub

Brian J. McCarthy

A MASTER CLASS IN VARIETY

Despite how skilled and sought after Brian J. McCarthy is as a designer, he didn't initially want to become one. His first ambition was to be a top equestrian, and he spent his youth in his hometown of Bethesda, Maryland, riding and eventually competing at the highest level. But this took its toll on him: "All I did was train and compete," he recalls. "I kind of felt like I had given up my life to do just that. I made a very conscious decision to let it go."

He then turned that same level of commitment and dedication to design: he rises at 4:30 a.m., leaving his partner, Danny Sager, and their little dog, Daisy, still snoozing; works out with a trainer; and is at his office, a block away from his midtown apartment, well before everyone else. This is less to do with energy, he explains, and more with a need for stimulation: "I get bored really easily. I don't want to look back and think, 'Oh God, I did this same thing here and here and here.'"

There is little chance of that. His interiors are a master class in variety and—above all else—quality. If there is a constant in his work, it's a love for luminosity, softly gleaming finishes, and translucence. In his own home, among his favorite objects is a pair of consoles by Claude Lalanne with upper sections of bronze crocodiles that look as if they have been melted and then draped on sinuous metal bases. The consoles flank the portal to the dining room and provide another design element McCarthy values: "a sense of entry." He bought his apartment in part because the main entryway satisfies his belief that a home needs an initial space that acts like a friendly introduction.

For all the high-end refinement in both his home and his designs, his rooms are always comfortable. Comfort is essential, something he learned when he took his first job with Parish-Hadley after studying at Pratt Institute, describing the design philosophy there as practical, sensible, and beautiful—in that order. And it was at Parish-Hadley where he learned a crucial lesson of his career: to restrain his earlier impulses to do too much in a space. This, he says, is one of the biggest mistakes decorators make.

McCarthy's living room is a considered mix of contemporary art, fine antiques, and unusual furnishings. A pair of bronze Crocodile consoles by Claude Lalanne flanks the opening to the dining room. A room-size custom rug from Beauvais pulls together the various seating areas.

Above: A second seating area in the living room mixes an armchair (right) by François-Honoré-Georges Jacob-Desmalter covered in velvet from Clarence House with a chair by Georges Jacob purchased in Paris. Beside the sofa, a bronze floor lamp by W. P. Sullivan stands near a painting by Guyana-born British artist Frank Bowling. "Always create a second seating area, when possible," says McCarthy. **Right:** In a corner of the dining room, a shaped-canvas work by Agostino Bonalumi hangs above a bronze console by Patrice Dangel.

Right: The dining room's deep-chocolate Venetian plaster walls by artisan Mark Giglio convey a feeling of intimacy. "I wanted a contrast between the white walls of the living room, sort of the white-black approach. It also acts like a dark mat for all the art in the room," says McCarthy. A bronze chandelier by Claude Lalanne hangs above a round glass-top table. Chairs in the style of Jean Royère are upholstered in a woven fabric by Toyine Sellers. **Below:** A large oil painting, *Menschenpemmikan* by Albert Oehlen, from Luhring Augustine gallery graces the walls of the room.

Left: In the master bedroom, a custom bed by Jonas, outfitted in embroidered linens from Julia B., stands on a rug from Beauvais. "I wanted the room to have a quiet feeling, a very deliberate absence of color," says McCarthy. The neutral walls also work as a perfect backdrop for the photographs, including a large work above the bed by George Rousse and a gelatin silver print by Minor White that hangs above a marble-topped bedside table. **Below:** An assortment of cufflinks is on display in a velvet tray. **Opposite:** A study that was a former guest bedroom mixes colorful art with antiques and a leopard-print carpet. A large work on paper by Mika Rottenberg leans against a wall covered in blueberry grass cloth from Phillip Jeffries. The small gilt bronze and marble side table is by Fernando and Humberto Campana and was purchased in London.

Q+A

with Brian J. McCarthy

In a few words, describe your design style.
Edited, classic, modern

What four designers/artists would you like to invite to dinner?
Henri Samuel, Albert Hadley, Bill Blass, and Francis Bacon

What are some of the design rules you've had to unlearn as you've become more experienced?
It's not a design rule, but steering away from getting caught in an academic approach to anything is something I talk a great deal about. I like spontaneity.

What's the simplest and best design rule?
Trust your instinct and follow your heart.

What's a design risk worth taking?
Something that takes you out of your comfort zone

How do you make your home feel welcoming?
Offer a drink as soon as guests arrive, for starters.

Where do you go for inspiration?
I keep my eyes wide open, and inspiration is always within eyesight.

What truly gives a home "life"?
For me it's the personal items that ultimately create a sort of scrapbook of our lives that give a home its energy and life.

How do you solve your storage problems?
Find a home for everything. Edit and discard when running out of space.

Do you really need all that stuff you have in storage?
We have very little in storage, because I believe it's better to give things to those in need than for those things to sit forgotten in storage.

Any preferences when it comes to your bed linens?
They must be crisp and cool. Always pressed and with a medium thread count.

How do you design around your pets?
I don't design around pets. There is nothing off limits to our dog. Mind you, I probably wouldn't choose a dog that sheds. But even then, I wouldn't necessarily design around that fact. Housekeeping would simply have to be diligent.

What do you covet but can't afford?
Paintings by Martin Kippenberger, Jean-Michel Basquiat, and Francis Bacon

What's your weekend routine?
We have a house in upstate New York. Decompressing up there after a week in the city is my weekend routine.

Do you wish you could spend more time at home?
Desperately! I am ultimately a homebody.

How long can you go without tidying up?
Not even a nanosecond

Do you have a treasured piece of clothing in your closet?
The tuxedo that my father wore when he married my mother

How do you make sure you enjoy your own parties?
By inviting interesting and authentic people

How do you subtly let guests know you want them to leave?
There is no subtle way. You just have to be brutally honest. Friends can handle it and always understand.

How do you stock a perfect bar?
Something for everyone. But for me, Belvedere vodka, Rose's lime juice, and a great white Burgundy.

What's your favorite cocktail?
Vodka gimlet

What sorts of things do you like to do the "old-fashioned" way?
Talking face to face or on the phone rather than e-mailing or texting

What's the worst thing about living in New York?
The relentless pace that one has to maintain to stay on top of your game.

What's the best thing about living in New York?
The access to anything that you can dream of. The exposure to culture and the arts is limitless, exciting, and inspiring.

What do you hope never changes in New York?
The diversity of its inhabitants

What small things make a bad New York day better?
Our dog, Daisy!

How do you get around town?
The quickest way possible! I use yellow cabs a lot, but sometimes the subway is the quickest and most efficient option.

Is there a particular place in the city that has a special meaning for you?
The Promenade in Brooklyn Heights. When I first moved to NYC to go to Pratt Institute, I lived near the campus on a student budget and I loved to treat myself to a piece of cheesecake from Sinclair's Bakery and sit on the Promenade and look at the Manhattan skyline and dream about my future.

Brian and Danny's rescue poodle, Daisy, is perched on a living room sofa.

Campion Platt

TAILORED, WITH AN EDGE

Above: In Platt's loft an LED lighting system diffuses a soft purple hue across the downstairs space. Platt designed the dining and living areas to flow together but when it came to the white lacquered kitchen he wanted it to be self-contained.
Opposite: A painting by Hunt Slonem hangs behind a delicate Swarovski crystal chandelier, which seems to float above a custom dining table and chairs.

Campion Platt believes that the best designs begin with learning as much as possible from the client, and then turning that information into a storyline that will flow throughout the residence. "You have to have a story before you can become inspired," he explains.

The story of his own apartment in SoHo was inspired by his wife, Tatiana. She always wanted a classic white downtown loft with exposed radiators and pipes, and although he wished to realize her dream, he told her that he would stick with the white floors and walls but "do a little more with it." The sleek penthouse where he lives with her and their four children is the result, one still loftlike in terms of the generous volumes of space but without a hard-edged industrial vibe.

"My wife actually didn't come to the apartment for eight months, until we moved in on July 4th. I cooked dinner for her and we ate on the terrace. We watched the fireworks, and she loved it. So we slept there that night, and the next night there was a torrential downpour. About two hundred gallons of water came in through a light fixture and destroyed everything, and we had to move out for four months."

The family did eventually get to call the place home, and although the apartment is very much a sophisticated and grown-up New York space, it's also designed with the children in mind—with durable fabrics, plenty of storage, and pleasing decorative objects that aren't too precious or breakable.

For Platt, luxury doesn't necessarily mean huge spaces, but fine craftsmanship that boasts opulent finishes such as leather, resin, and marble. Trained as an architect at Columbia University, he spent years designing compact spaces and believes that with the right finishes and built-ins they can be as luxurious as something grander in scale. And whereas he is passionate about all aspects of design, Platt enjoys the early stages best, when he sketches out his first set of ideas. Process, he says, is ultimately more gratifying than seeing all the pieces put into place.

Above: In the living room, glamour is not sacrificed for family comfort. A plush sheepskin rug and soft purple and cream fabrics flow together around the distinctive backlit monolithic ebony fireplace that also houses a recessed flat-screen television. **Right:** White-lacquer illuminated shelves display carefully edited objects and photography. **Opposite:** Platt organized the loft's voluminous footprint and massive fifteen-foot-high ceilings by dividing the space into "virtual rooms" that each have distinct functions. A separate lounge area complete with an *L*-shaped banquette and floor-to-ceiling bookshelves was carved out of a front corner of the living room.

Left: Upstairs Platt designed a spacious refuge for himself and his wife, Tatiana, with separate areas for relaxing, sleeping, and working. A fireplace, retractable ceiling shades, and furnishings are in soft colors. These areas open up to a large outdoor terrace. **Below:** A wall of custom built-ins serves as an upstairs office for Tatiana.

Left: Platt softened the all-white walls of the seating area by using a mixture of feminine pinks and a flower-patterned rug by Fort Street Studio. **Below:** An upholstered pink linen-velvet wall creates a romantic, cocoon-like feeling in the sleeping area of the master suite.

Q+A
with Campion Platt

In a few words, describe your design style.
Fresh and crisp with an edge and a sense of humor

What four designers would you like to invite to dinner?
Carlo Mollino, Carlo Scarpa, Gio Ponti, and Antonio Sant'Elia—all eating black squid-ink pasta

What would your perfect room look like?
A room derived from the set in the ending scenes of *2001: A Space Odyssey*

What are some of the design rules you've had to unlearn as you've become more experienced?
Rules are meant to be broken for truly inspired design.

What's your best budget-friendly design hack?
Furniture from GloDea

What's a design risk worth taking?
Working away from your sweet spot and letting go of old standards

How do you make your home feel welcoming?
Keeping it fresh and fun with good art and lots of reclining areas

Tell us ways that you've used lighting to resolve a dark room.
Atmospheric wall-washing lighting or hidden in coves; not many point sources

Where do you go for inspiration?
Traveling and art museums

What truly gives a home "life"?
My kids joking around with me, playing music, and telling stories

How do you solve your storage problems?
Design lots of built-ins and throw out stuff regularly

Do you really need all that stuff you have in storage?
No, and it's also on my mind to take care of . . . five storage places in three cities.

Any preferences when it comes to your bed linens?
Thread count lower than 400 and no duvet

What do you covet but can't afford?
Lots of Légers and de Chiricos

What's the best way to start the day?
A warm child's snuggle and morning meditation

What smells of home for you?
Hamptons salt air and lavender in the garden

What's your weekend routine?
Morning ocean swim with kids and homemade gluten-free granola, except in New York, where the East River is not people friendly

How long can you go without tidying up?
Way too long, unfortunately. Clean desks make clean minds.

Where is your favorite place in the apartment to take a nap?
Corner lounge *L*-shape sofa under a soft sun

Do you have a treasured piece of clothing in your closet?
Lots of custom Moroccan suits that I can rarely find the right occasion for

How do you make sure you enjoy your own parties?
By cooking great food to be enjoyed by all

How do you subtly let guests know you want them to leave?
I leave

How do you stock a perfect bar?
Kombucha. I don't drink.

What sorts of things do you like to do the "old-fashioned" way?
Outdoor showers

What's the best thing about living in New York?
An endless renewal of culture, art, and community, and changing neighborhoods, finding something new on an old well-known street

What's the worst thing about living in New York?
There is no worst thing. Most people dream of living in New York at some point.

What do you hope never changes in New York?
Rockefeller Center

What small things make a bad New York day better?
Rain at 4 p.m., so I can take a nap before dinner

How do you get around town?
Citi Bike or subway. If they are unavailable, I take a taxi before Uber or Lyft, to support the TLC [Taxi & Limousine Commission].

Is there a particular place in the city that has a special meaning for you?
Raoul's, where I met my wife

A separate dressing area includes a well-organized, spacious closet showcasing Tatiana's extensive shoe collection.

Howard Slatkin

WARM OPULENCE

Howard Slatkin's residence on "upper, upper, upper Fifth Avenue" was his thirtieth birthday present to himself, and what he calls "a handyman's special." In other words, it was a total gut job. The apartment is truly one of the city's most special interiors—a complete and intricate labor of love. Every single object, surface, work of art, and piece of furniture has been chosen with such felt affection that despite the apparent opulence, the apartment is not overwhelming but full of warmth and wonderfully inviting.

Having said that, Slatkin keeps a low profile and sees privacy as the last great luxury. Only close friends and family are entertained in his homes, and it was only under pressure from others, particularly his beloved late mother, that he wound up having the apartment photographed at all. This is one of the few published examples of his design, since he only works for select clients who share similar values of privacy. "I've never sought the limelight and I've never needed it. I like doing my work and leading my little life. I'm not very social and all of that." He doesn't consider himself shy, however, and simply says that he is content to live a life that is unrecorded, which shouldn't be considered so very remarkable.

But his design *is* remarkable, even if he isn't formally trained, but informed by obsessive reading and research as well as a passion for the European exquisite. "I was a designer for two years before I knew there was a D&D building. [Sister] Parish told me about it." Parish also asked him to join her at Parish-Hadley when he was only twenty-three years old, but he has always gone solo, detouring into other businesses along the way, including owning a store and cofounding a home fragrance brand.

The whole renovation process took precisely thirty-three months, and, ever the perfectionist, Slatkin's eye still falls "on what I did wrong and what I would do differently today." But ultimately, he put his heart and soul into this little palace. "I know that I have very nice things, and I know that I'm blessed."

No detail has been overlooked in Slatkin's exquisite living room. "I wanted a living room that was large enough to accommodate a dozen people but be equally comfortable for me alone," he explains. The sweeping Central Park views were the main source of inspiration when choosing a wall color. Slatkin settled on cool shades of a pale chalky gray and mauve, which he calls "cloud."

Above: A banquette runs the full length of a seating area off the main living room. An aviary of porcelain birds is arranged on the coffee table, and Chinese export birds are perched on top of gilt wood brackets fitted with recessed lighting. **Left:** In the library, leather panels provide a harmonious background for the furniture and objects. Against the far wall an assortment of rock-crystal candlesticks is arranged on top of an eighteenth-century ebony-brass-and-tortoiseshell bureau. **Opposite:** A French Empire Savonnerie carpet had just the right colors and neoclassical design Slatkin had in mind when planning the decor for the dining room. The exquisite panels and ceiling, hand-painted by Sasha Solodukho and his team, were inspired by Raphael's loggia at the Vatican.

Right: "I am a proponent of open storage," says Slatkin. He decided that he wanted his dressing room to feel like an inlaid marquetry wood box, covering the walls and ceiling with an assortment of real wood veneers and trompe l'oeil.
Below: The bedroom walls are a combination of three different patterns, designed to work together in the same gray-blue, taupe, and ivory colors. To give the prints an extra dimension, Slatkin had the fabric embroidered by the Paris workroom of Jean-François Lesage. A mahogany-and-brass Russian bed is surrounded by paintings and drawings collected over the years.

Above: "As I like having friends visit in the bedroom, I always furnish it with a sofa," says Slatkin. The designer had a Louis XVI canapé upholstered in Le Manach's emerald-green silk-velvet and then, for extra luxury, hand-quilted. Draped over the back is a blanket made out of an old sable coat that once belonged to Slatkin's mother. The midcentury lamps with cellulose shades sit on a pair of Chinese-style Louis XVI mahogany tables. **Right:** Panels of eighteenth-century Chinese wallpaper were the inspiration for the guest bedroom. "I knew I wanted to create a room in which my guests would feel that they were spending the night in a magical garden," explains Slatkin. The French Empire steel-and-gilt-bronze lit à la polonaise has a canopy of Indian printed-voile scarves.

Q+A

with Howard Slatkin

In a few words, describe your design style.
A mixed bag of a souk, filled with what I love. Hopefully with comfort and a sense of quality.

What four designers would you like to invite to dinner?
My two mentors who taught me so much at the start of my career: Renzo Mongiardino and Henri Samuel. And at this fantasy dinner I would include Pablo Picasso and Leonardo da Vinci.

What would your perfect room look like?
Like the rooms I have for myself—comfortable, good lighting to read by, a table wherever one sits to put down a drink, flowers, fireplace, and lots of books—surrounded by beauty.

What are some of the design rules you've had to unlearn as you've become more experienced?
That the client is always right.

What's your best budget-friendly design hack?
Buy things of quality and beauty to the degree you can—things of quality never have to be replaced.

What's the simplest and best design rule?
Only have what you love and always do what is suitable—for where you live and how you live.

What's a design risk worth taking?
Breaking any conceived "rule."

How do you make your home feel welcoming?
Beautiful scent in every room, flowers from the garden or greenhouses, a roaring fire, a stocked bar, and very comfortable seating, and places wherever one sits to read or put down a drink, and flattering light, and beautiful views. And delicious homemade food. It's quite simple.

Where do you go for inspiration?
Great novels—the great writers create worlds with words that are far more inspirational than actual rooms and certainly more than photographs of rooms, which are often flat. And great pictures can inspire colors, patterns, or new ideas.

How do you solve your storage problems?
Edit. If I don't love it, it gets passed on.

Do you really need all that stuff you have in storage?
Of course not—we need nothing. But some things are hard to resist because they are so beautiful, especially

pictures and it can be exciting to rotate them, like having a friend come back for a visit.

Any preferences when it comes to your bed linens?
Wrinkled sheets are not allowed. And bed linens changed daily.

How do you design around your pets?
By putting their needs and comfort first and foremost—that they can easily get on every chair, sofa, and bed. That they have vistas to look at. And have water bowls—refilled throughout the day—in several locations.

What have you broken that you still mourn?
I mourn for no material things—broken, lost, or stolen. Life is too short to even think about them. All material things are replaceable.

What's the best way to start the day?
By the gentle nudging of a dog who wants to go out

What job would you be terrible at?
Anything that would require lying—so I guess that means politics.

What kind of music do you listen to at home?
Depends on my mood, but most often classical. I also like classic country.

What smells of home for you?
Seasonal scents, be they from the garden or scented candles—paperwhites in December, roses in June, the ocean in July and August . . .

What's the first thing you do when you come home from a trip?
Wonder why I ever left

What's your weekend routine?
The same as my weekday.

How long can you go without tidying up?

Luckily I have people who do it for me—but I like rooms to be rather untidy. Tidy rooms are a bore.

Do you have a treasured piece of clothing in your closet?
If it fits, it's treasured.

How do you make sure you enjoy your own parties?
Only have friends you long to be with—that is the most important element. I never have anyone who is not a close friend come to my home. And all aspects must be natural and a reflection of your lifestyle, nothing forced or overwrought or unnatural—just an extension of how you live your daily life, the same food, the same dishes, et cetera.

How do you subtly let guests know you want them to leave?
My guests are only very good friends, so I have no problem with telling them it's time to go—but rarely do they not know when the party is over.

What sorts of things do you like to do the "old-fashioned" way?
Probably just about everything.

Coins, foulards, and other various sundries are stored in bowls and open baskets in the dressing room.

Sheila Bridges

ARTFUL NESTING

It's no surprise Sheila Bridges ended up as what she terms a "professional nester," because she's a homebody at heart. That hasn't stopped her from leading a flourishing design business and diversifying into both television and writing. Nor did she hesitate to publish her memoir, *The Bald Mermaid*, which unflinchingly chronicles relationships both happy and lousy, the ultimately empowering experience of losing her hair to alopecia, and the challenges of working in an industry where there are very few African Americans.

Bridges grew up in Pennsylvania, attended a Quaker school, and studied at both Brown University and Parsons School of Design before moving to Harlem more than twenty years ago, well before the recent wave of gentrification. After the first round of renovations on her airy, graceful apartment, which included painting most of the walls a soft, creamy white, the palette shifted to distilled blues, moss green, and a shot of ripe tangerine that makes the entryway pack a punch. When Bill Clinton decided to locate his post-presidential offices in Harlem, Bridges was hired to decorate them, an experience that involved going shopping after hours with the Secret Service in tow.

Although she spends a lot of time in her Hudson Valley residence with her horses and dogs, Harlem remains an inspiration. After searching for just the right wallpaper for her country house, she finally came up with her own design, which she calls "Harlem Toile de Jouy." The design has since been acquired for the permanent collections of several museums, including the Cooper Hewitt and the Musée de la Toile de Jouy. Having always loved traditional French toile of the late 1700s, she subverted the traditional pastoral motifs, her intent being, in part, to "lampoon stereotypes deeply woven into the African American experience." This thoughtful and historically informed approach is evident throughout her apartment. On the other hand, she's straightforward about twentieth-century objects such as music systems and televisions. "They are what they are, so show them."

On Bridges's living room walls, Farrow & Ball's Oval Room Blue creates a soft-hued background for her collection of Swedish country furniture. "I initially painted the entire apartment in white, but when I lived in the space for a while and evolved as a designer I introduced more color." A formal seating area weaves in pieces from travels such as an inlaid Moroccan table that stands near a Gustavian clock.

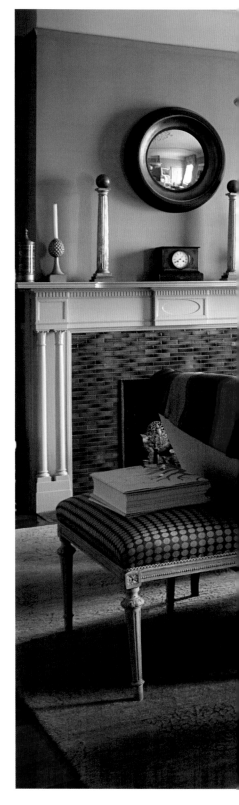

Right: Another seating area in the living room is a balance of lightly layered colors and styles. Brightly colored faux-tortoise boxes add a pop of color to a Swedish desk. An Empire marble-top table stands beside a custom club chair covered in Holland & Sherry fabric. **Below:** In the apple-green dining room, Bridges combined two demilune tables to form a single table and completed the look with a set of French chairs, with seats upholstered in leather and backs upholstered in green silk. **Below right:** A hallway is enlivened with Bridges's Van Doe wallpaper, where a deer stands in as the subject of many famous paintings.

Right: In a corner of Bridges's bedroom, a mannequin displays her collection of jewelry and antique bags from her grandmother. The walls, hand-painted by Pintura Studio, are filled with family photographs and art that she made as a child. **Below:** A Swedish bedside chest and a small side chair are positioned next to the bed. "I gravitate toward Gustavian furniture. It has a lightness that gives flexibility when designing around it," says Bridges.

Q+A
with Sheila Bridges

In a few words, describe your design style.
Classic, colorful, edgy, and eclectic. I love mixing more traditional styles and silhouettes with modern art.

Which four designers would you like to invite to dinner?
Brian McCarthy, Joy Moyler, Christopher Coleman, and Jean-Michel Frank (ghost guest)

What would your perfect room look like?
Spacious, timeless, comfortable, and colorful. It's my living room.

What are some of the design rules you've had to unlearn as you've become more experienced?
Just because it looks great in a plan or elevation doesn't mean that it works in reality.

What's your best budget-friendly design hack?
Marble and ceramic tile from Home Depot

What's the simplest and best design rule?
Design is a thoughtful process that takes time.

What's a design risk worth taking?
As an interior designer and product designer, I consider all design a risk worth taking.

How do you make your home feel welcoming?
By leaving colorful Moroccan babouches in the entry and telling guests to take off their shoes

Where do you go for inspiration?
I travel—Iceland, Africa, Paris, Berlin—anywhere and everywhere.

What truly gives a home "life"?
Personal touches such as photographs, accessories, and art—things that truly reflect who you are

How do you solve your storage problems?
Lots of bins

Do you really need all that stuff you have in storage?
No. Like most designers, I suffer from what I call "acquisition disorder," but I'm determined to get rid of these storage units this year. Guess I should open another store!

Any preferences when it comes to your bed linens?
Yes, I love crisp white bed linens. I won't buy anything else. I'm convinced that patterns give me nightmares!

How do you design around your pets?
My pets are family, but I train them rather than design around them.

What do you covet but can't afford?
A Kerry James Marshall oil painting

What's the best way to start the day?
A walk in Central Park with my two Australian shepherds

Long hot soak in the tub or quick shower?
A hot soak with bath salts followed by a cool shower

What job would you be terrible at?
Candy shop owner. I would eat all of the merchandise.

What kind of music do you listen to at home?
A mix of pretty much everything, but hip hop, soul, and jazz in heavy rotation

How long can you go without tidying up?
About fifteen minutes

Do you wish you could spend more time at home?
Yes, I consider myself a homebody.

What's your weekend routine?
It depends on the season, but most weekends are spent upstate in the Hudson Valley. If the weather is good, it usually includes the farmers' market in the morning, tennis with friends or a trainer, a walk/hike with my dogs, a visit to the barn to see my retired quarter horse Red, and anything else that involves the outdoors.

Where is your favorite place in the apartment to take a nap?
My bed. I'm a professional nap taker. There is no such thing as a "cat nap."

How do you make sure you enjoy your own parties?
I hire a caterer so that I can enjoy spending time with guests instead of being stuck in the kitchen.

What's the best thing about living in New York?
I never get bored.

What's the worst thing about living in New York?
The filth, the crowds, and the constant reminder of the disparity of wealth in this country

What do you hope never changes in New York?
The 24/7 energy

What small things make a bad New York day better?
The ability to just walk into a museum and catch an amazing exhibition on a whim

Is there a particular place in the city that has a special meaning for you?
Harlem—the neighborhood I call home.

A round tufted sofa is the focal point in Bridges's tangerine-colored entrance hall.

Timothy Whealon

STRIKING A BALANCE

There was once the possibility that Timothy Whealon would become an English literature professor. There was also the possibility that he would become a Wall Street banker or some kind of corporate manager at a major auction house. He may yet become a writer, but at present he is most definitely a designer.

Brought up in the Midwest, Whealon was educated at Kenyon College, where his dissertation on James Baldwin, and presumably his all-around academic performance, led to a possible teaching fellowship. But he decided against academia and instead chose a "sensible" career path in finance. "I must have been delusional or something," he says, "but I did learn accounting, and can understand a balance sheet." He left Wall Street after six months and completed two rigorous training programs at Sotheby's, both in London and New York; a salient feature of his work, which is very much rooted in classicism, is his knowledge of international arts and antiques. In 1994, he founded his own firm.

Whealon's Gramercy Park penthouse apartment with its wraparound terrace is testament to the soothing symmetry of his design sensibility. His impeccable taste, however, stays far away from sterility—"Something has to be off balance." The rooms of his apartment, while crisply detailed to perfection, are still welcoming and bright, filled with light that pours in on all sides. Things cohere and flow; the same Calacatta marble that is used in the bathroom is used in the kitchen, and the greenery outside on the terrace is reflected inside through a subtle green-and-white color scheme. It's a place where Whealon can actually relax. "I can spend a whole day in the apartment just reading or watching a documentary. I have a personality that is part introvert, part extrovert, perhaps like all of us."

Whealon's penthouse apartment is filled with light that streams in from a large wraparound terrace packed with greenery. While the design and color schemes are quite formal and carefully disciplined, the end result is light and joyful. The pair of cane chairs were designed by Pierre Jeanneret. A bust of Minerva sits on top of a campaign chest that was purchased from a Palm Beach antiques store; the walls are lined with photographs and prints by such artists as Ellsworth Kelly, Gerhard Richter, and Rineke Dijkstra.

150

Above: Striking a balance between modern and classic, Whealon furnished the living room with a custom sofa inspired by a Billy Baldwin design and covered in a Christopher Farr textile. The cocktail table, also a custom design, stands on an Abaca rug from Merida. The flat-screen television is recessed into a wall of bookshelves, which also displays a collection of abalone currency rings from New Guinea. **Right:** A sleekly compact kitchen is tucked into a corner of the main living space. The lacquer cabinetry is custom made; the backsplash and countertop are Calacatta marble.

Above: The south-facing wall of Whealon's bedroom displays works of art by such artists as Kiki Smith, Ellsworth Kelly, and Gabriel Orozco. A ceramic sculpture by Eva Hild is displayed on an Italian inlaid fruitwood commode. **Left:** Bedtime reading is stacked beneath a Chinese lacquered tea stand. Swing-arm sconces hang above a custom-made bed upholstered in an Amanda Nisbet Design fabric.

153

The apartment and terrace, which has multiple entertaining areas, are a small slice of paradise away from the hurly-burly of city life. "I love having nothing to do. It's my favorite thing," says Whealon.

Q+A
with Timothy Whealon

In a few words, describe your design style.
Worldly, edited, classic . . . rooted in the past and sprouted in the present

What four designers would you like to invite to dinner?
Frances Elkins, Diego Giacometti, David Hicks, and Jacques Grange

What would your perfect room look like?
It would have great classical architecture, soaring ceilings, floor-to-ceiling windows with a view, and lots of natural light, contemporary art, a mix of antique and modern furnishings . . . and open onto outdoor space, of course!

What are some of the design rules you've had to unlearn as you've become more experienced?
Small rooms look bigger with larger-scale furniture. I'm a symmetry freak, but you always have to throw something off in order to make it balanced.

What's your best budget-friendly design hack?
Bleach it or paint it white!

What's the simplest and best design rule?
Keep it authentic to yourself and the place.

What's a design risk worth taking?
Pattern on pattern

Tell us ways that you've used lighting to resolve a dark room.
A mix of ambient and direct lighting. Sconces, picture lights, and beautifully crafted vellum lampshades always help.

How do you make your home feel welcoming?
I fill it with my own personality and spray it with orange blossom.

How do you solve your storage problems?
I have three storage units, so I obviously have not been successful in solving this problem.

Do you really need all the stuff you have in storage?
It depends if you are talking about my storage facility in the Hamptons or my two in the city.

Any preferences when it comes to your bed linens?
They must be cold, crisp, and beautifully pressed with lavender spray.

What's the best way to start the day?
With some gratitude, a positive thought, the *New York Times*, and a little coffee from Sant Ambroeus.

What kind of music do you listen to at home?
I run the gamut from Eminem, Norah Jones, and Shawn Mendes to Vivaldi . . . and I'm also a closet Carpenters and Neil Diamond listener.

What smells of home for you?
As an adult, orange blossom. As a childhood memory, freshly brewed coffee and cinnamon rolls baking in the oven.

How long can you go without tidying up?
Hmmmm . . . let me think long and hard about that question . . . maybe a millisecond?

Where is your favorite place to take a nap?
On the terrace sofa . . .

Do you have a treasured piece of clothing in your closet?
My father's 1970s camel-hair jacket with its original leather buttons.

How do you subtly let guests know you want them to leave?
I go to bed!

How do you stock a perfect bar?
With great attention to detail!

What's your favorite cocktail?
Margarita with fresh squeezed lime

What sorts of things do you like to do the "old-fashioned" way?
Whiskey!

What's the best thing about living in New York?
I'm never bored!

What do you hope never changes in New York?

The view from my terrace and the city's diversity

What small things make a bad New York day better?
Laughter and a small kindness!

How do you get around town?
With my own Waze navigation app . . . even when someone else is driving

Is there a particular place in the city that has a special meaning for you?
I'm a downtown guy, but Central Park holds a special place in my heart.

Ollie, Whealon's Ganaraskan, enjoying the sunlight on the penthouse terrace

David Kleinberg

OLD WORLD, NEW STYLE

Above and opposite: In the dining room, Kleinberg maintained the space's jewel-box feeling by keeping the existing Denning & Fourcade lacquered chinoiserie panels. He updated the room with new light fixtures, 1940s chairs, and a light wood table, and added some extra glamour by hanging a red lacquered frame on a mirrored wall above the marble fireplace mantle.

David Kleinberg's small but perfectly formed Upper East Side apartment, as elegant as its owner, is filled with lovely soft light and complete with a particular kind of living room he had long been searching for: quietly grand with tall windows, high ceilings, and good light. Such rooms are usually only found in large, astronomically priced apartments, so he was delighted when he eventually found one in an affordable space. The apartment, however, had a great deal of faux bois, damask, and curtain-smothered windows, a look he describes as "very Denning & Fourcade."

Kleinberg uses this description fondly because that was where he got his first summer job after studying at Trinity College in Hartford, Connecticut. He remembers the renowned decorating pair as wonderfully eccentric men who were "full-on Napoleon III" in their approach to style, and he credits them for teaching him the value of fanciful thought. He went on to work at Parish-Hadley for some sixteen years and realized that the clean, classic taste so beautifully realized by Albert Hadley was also where his heart lay.

Although the faux bois and the heavy curtains were banished, Kleinberg kept the Denning & Fourcade lacquered chinoiserie panels in the dining room. Together with orchids on the original marble mantel and an alabaster Art Deco light fixture, the room is exotically intimate for dinner parties, which he doesn't cook for. He last cooked—reportedly a single lamb chop—when he was twenty-two, just after he finished college, moved away from Great Neck, Long Island, where he grew up, and rented a fifth-floor walk-up studio on 64th Street. In addition to not cooking, Kleinberg neither paints nor draws: "I'm the least artistic person in this business." Needless to say, his design career belies this.

Kleinberg, a total Francophile, shelved books for two years in a public library to save money for his first trip to Paris at the age of sixteen. "I remember walking through the Left Bank toward the river and literally weeping." He once thought that a move to Paris was a distinct possibility, perhaps in retirement—"I don't want to be doing this until I'm ninety," he explains. Kleinberg is one of the few decorators who seems to actually contemplate retirement, but the appeal of his apartment is, after having lived in quite a few different places over the years, a feeling that he's really found his home. "Maybe I'll just sit in this nice room and read a book."

Right, below, and below right: The living room with its lofty ceilings and oversize windows accommodates multiple seating areas. The elaborate millwork was painted in various shades of white to give the room extra luminosity. An acrylic-and-gouache painting by Garth Weiser hangs above a chocolate linen-velvet custom sofa. A pair of Danish neoclassical chairs are arranged near a coffee table by Jean Royère. A Bruno Romeda circular sculpture stands front and center on the coffee table. The graceful 1937 corkscrew chandelier was made by the Swiss modernist Max Ernst Haefeli.

Left: The master bedroom is outfitted in calming neutral tones. A custom bed is topped with an E. Braun & Co. coverlet, and a pale carpet from Patterson Flynn Martin complements the striped linen fabric on the walls and the matching curtains. The ceramic vessel is from Primavera.

Right: In the kitchen, chunky Calacatta marble countertops mix with vintage stainless-steel cabinets. The standing candelabra is by Erik Höglund.

Above and opposite: In the study, Kleinberg designed an off-white linen and green flannel sectional sofa to double as a guest bed with a queen-size pullout mattress. He covered the walls with linen panels trimmed with nailheads. The marble-and-mahogany table was found on the website 1stdibs. Facing the sofa, a pair of Edward Wormley chairs are covered in leather from J. Robert Scott.

Q+A
with David Kleinberg

In a few words, describe your design style.
Based in tradition and filtered through the lens of modern experience—it is, I hope, of this time and not faddish. I strive in my design to achieve a balance between comfort, style, and suitability.

Name a past designer, artist, or creative who has had the most influence on your style.
Albert Hadley. Sixteen years of apprenticeship and working together was invaluable and shaped my aesthetic in every way possible.

What would your perfect room look like?
A double cube with enormous windows on all sides. From each window you would see a perfect but different landscape, the ocean from one, the mountains from another, open fields, and a city skyline from the other two—a vision of the world from one place.

What's the simplest and best design rule?
Edit!

What's a design risk worth taking?
One that takes you out of your comfort zone—you will see things in a new and unexpected way.

How do you make your home feel welcoming?
By smiling when I open the door

Where do you go for inspiration?
I travel for inspiration. Next stop is Japan, where I haven't been for thirty-five years.

What truly gives a home "life"?
Laughter truly brings life to a home.

How do you solve your storage problems?
That's easy. I throw things away. I am ruthless about clutter.

Do you really need all that stuff you have in storage?
I don't have storage (see above)!

What do you covet but can't afford?
I covet deeply a private jet.

What's the best way to start the day?
Best way to start the day is to be on holiday.

Long hot soak in the tub or quick shower?
Quick hot shower

What job would you be terrible at?
I would be a terrible waiter.

What smells of home for you?
Christian Tortu's Forets (Forest) candles

What's the first thing you do when you come home from a trip?
I read my mail.

What's your weekend routine?
In the summers my weekend routine is to take the seaplane out to East Hampton, exercise, see friends, garden, eat homemade meals using as much from the vegetable garden as possible, and breathe deep.

How long can you go without tidying up?
I must admit that I am a neat freak so I can't go a minute without tidying up; it drives everyone around me to distraction. Never leave a newspaper unattended in my presence.

Where is your favorite place to take a nap?
Who takes a nap?

Do you have a treasured piece of clothing in your closet?
I try not to treasure things.

How do you make sure you enjoy your own parties?
I make sure everything is ready well in advance, so I can be with my guests and not in the kitchen.

How do you subtly let guests know you want them to leave?
I don't think I ever want my guests to leave.

What's your favorite cocktail?
A very dry vodka martini with one olive

What sorts of things do you like to do the "old-fashioned" way?
I take notes the old-fashioned way, on a 5x7 yellow lined pad; I can't get used to notes on my iPhone.

What's the best thing about living in New York?
The diversity

What's the worst thing about living in New York?
The endless construction

What do you hope never changes in New York?
I hope the momentum of New York never changes.

How do you get around town?
I get around town in my Range Rover, which is driven slightly too fast by my driver, Alan, who knows I am always running late.

Is there a particular place in the city that has a special meaning for you?
The old Four Seasons restaurant had special meaning to me—wonderful Thanksgiving dinners for many years with a close group of friends. Sadly, that restaurant is not the same any more.

Kleinberg created an intriguing barrel-vaulted main hallway by covering the surfaces in Venetian plaster.

Thomas Jayne

CABINETS OF CURIOSITIES

Thomas Jayne loves the way Benjamin Franklin wore his Quaker coat with a red lining. This observation sums up Jayne, who has quirk, quality, and perhaps most importantly, a strong sense of history. As much a historian as a designer, his work draws on a deep knowledge of period architecture and the decorative arts. For him, everything is connected, and the fluent play of past and present within the beautiful rooms he creates is a testament to what he calls his very traditional but very enlightened education. This included attending an Episcopal day school in Pacific Palisades, Los Angeles, where he grew up.

Jayne remembers his childhood as being very colorful and filled with eccentric, stylish people. "After school, I used to visit the cacti and succulent editor for *Sunset* magazine. She once arranged a bowl of lemons that had fallen, so they were this wonderful brown-lemon color," he recalls. "We grew lemons and I thought I should bring her some fresh ones, but she said she preferred the color of the old ones. I loved that."

Degrees in architecture and the allied arts, stints at Christie's and the J. Paul Getty Museum, and a fellowship at the American Wing of the Metropolitan Museum of Art preceded Jayne's design career, which began when he went to work for Parish-Hadley. His background may indeed be scholarly, but while his rooms are elegant and thoughtful, there is a sense of morbid humor in them as well. One room in his SoHo loft—which he shares with his husband, writer and food stylist Richmond Ellis—is designated "the cabinet room" because it's a cabinet of curiosities: a raven perches on an ornate pedestal, South African fox bats are suspended from the pressed-tin ceiling, and a nineteenth-century Black Forest bear statue clutches a collection of canes.

The couple hosts an annual Halloween party and regular Sunday roasts, and, because they love New Orleans where they also have a home, they often serve gumbo and jambalaya. "We light the chandeliers, lay out my grandmother's damask tablecloths, and invite what we call our unofficial family."

A floating wall of bookcases in Jayne's loft acts as a partition, which includes a pair of colored glass doors that opens into a space called the cabinet room.

YEAH
YEAH
BLUR
THE
ZOMIES
CAMEL
JOAN
RIVERS
1977
COULTRAIN
MARILAN
THE CURE
SMITH
BLUE
CHEER
JOE BOUYS

Above: In the main seating area, furniture is arranged below a skylight that is lined with yellow-colored mirror. A pair of eighteenth-century Chinese root wood chairs sits on top of a large Isfahan carpet. **Right:** The dining area has an American sideboard and a bust of George Washington by Jean-Antoine Houdon, one in a group of busts of patriots placed around the loft. The yellow-mirror wall, an homage to Sir John Soane and his London house museum, adds a touch of bright luminosity. A nineteenth-century table is surrounded by old and new chairs. "The mix summarizes the aesthetic of the loft," says Jayne.

168

Left: The cabinet room holds a concentration of small sculptures, found objects, and specimens of natural history. "They would have looked lost if we spread them all around the apartment," says Jayne. A portrait of his mother hangs above a desk that once belonged to his grandmother and is thought to be fashioned from a piano. **Below left:** The Victorian bed once belonged to Jayne's grandparents. "Heavy Victorian furniture can be a challenge, but I was able to lighten it up by framing it in a yellow color block," he says. **Below:** An antique chest with religious relics and a mirror by Oriel Harwood are flanked by a pair of lavender bookcases.

Q+A
with Thomas Jayne

In a few words, describe your design style.
Up-to-date, traditional, or [a mixture of] anything after the Renaissance

Name a past designer, artist, or creative who has had the most influence on your style.
Thomas Chippendale, Rose Cumming, Ray and Charles Eames, Rick Ellis, and Henry Francis du Pont

What are some of the design rules you've had to unlearn as you've become more experienced?
The rules have only become more enforced for me. Design is about contrasts—subtle and arch—and that is always the question. We need to always look for these contrasts. I am reexamining cool colors after a career with warm ones.

What's your best budget-friendly design hack?
Color. It is usually the same price to have something an interesting color as a boring one. Cool is free, I like to say.

What's the simplest and best design rule?
Simplicity and maybe a bit of decorative flourish—think of the best Chippendale furniture.

What's a design risk worth taking?
All great design engenders risk and invention. In a traditional mien, risk is essential.

Tell us ways that you've used lighting to resolve a dark room.
Dark walls in a dark apartment are an asset—it plays up the light sources that are there. And we are enjoying a revival of uplights—we think of Paige Rense every time we use them.

How do you make your home feel welcoming?
Comfortable places to stand and sit—always key and essential. Personality in objects and decor always makes a welcoming room.

What truly gives a home "life"?
People

How do you solve your storage problems?
Edit until everything fits. We have a ton of storage.

What do you covet but can't afford?
I think I have pretty much everything I want save a retirement account that will last until I am 110. My biggest fear is running out of red beans and rice (with sausage) in New Orleans.

What have you broken that you still mourn?
Not much in this transitory life. Maybe a lifetime of Christmas ornaments melting in a flood, and before my eyes—Christmas decorating was my first professional design work.

What's the best way to start the day?
Coffee in bed. Then the gym, aka physical therapy or the temple of vanity

What smells of home for you?
Cantaloupe

What's the first thing you do when you come home from a trip?
Put my wallet on my great-grandfather's chest of drawers

What's your weekend routine?
Physical education. Farmers' market. Saint Mary's and roast chicken on Sunday night. And usually one cultural activity: a museum, a movie, et cetera. And making the big list for the following week.

Do you wish you could spend more time at home?
Yes. There are stacks of unexamined books. We need a fortnight lockdown just for the library.

How do you make sure you enjoy your own parties?
Lots of preplanning and help, careful consideration of guests, leftovers

How do you stock a perfect bar?
With whatever my friends are drinking. Gin for Albert. Vodka for Alphonso. Champagne for all. Luxardo cherries for Manhattans.

What's your favorite cocktail?
Rum punch—reminds me of Peter Pennoyer and our projects in Maine

What sorts of things do you like to do the "old-fashioned" way?

Hand-tie bow ties, notes that are handwritten, arts and crafts, and saying good morning to strangers

What's the best thing about living in New York?
New York is the home to as many as eight hundred languages.

What's the worst thing about living in New York?
There are not drawbacks . . . but being from the West, I miss outdoor space.

What do you hope never changes in New York?
I hope there is some charm here when I die.

How do you get around town?
All modes of transportation, including bicycle

Is there a particular place in the city that has a special meaning for you?
The Battery and the Church of Saint Mary the Virgin

The loft, which Jayne shares with his partner, Rick, is filled with furniture, paintings, sculpture, architectural fragments, and models acquired in their more than thirty years together.

Sara Story

COMFORTS OF THE EXOTIC

Above: Story's town house reflects her Texas-size personality and her ability to infuse liveliness into a home. A disco ball–style fixture from Soane hangs near a sculptural white staircase by architect Alan Orenbuch. **Opposite:** A portrait of Story by Will Cotton perfectly captures her sense of fun.

Raised in Texas, Sara Story was born in Japan and lived with her family for several years in both Thailand and Singapore. A love of Asian cultures still has a strong hold over her and emerges in her design in ways both subtle and obvious.

Whereas her work for clients is often subdued, in her own home, a large and lovely town house on Gramercy Park, her exploration of an Eastern aesthetic is much more lively: slippers from India are lined up by the front door; the library color scheme is a dramatic Chinese red and black; floor tiles from Marrakesh enliven a guest bathroom; and lacquered finishes, rugs from Istanbul, and a row of pensive Thai monks stand before a fireplace. Vibrant modern art, meanwhile, striking contemporary chandeliers, and a sculptural and sinuous white staircase prevent the whole space from becoming overly themed.

Story has three school-age children, but that doesn't stop her from traveling as often as every six weeks to escape New York: "I have to go somewhere, even to Paris for two nights." If they are not in school, she takes the kids and two nannies with her, even to the King's Cup in Thailand, an elephant polo tournament in which she participates every September. "It's just like these crazy people from around the world . . . India, Nepal. It's totally fun."

Design is also meant to be fun, she says. What should be taken seriously is the business side of things. "I would say the creative part is 20 percent and the business part is 80 percent." This is something she learned while working at Victoria Hagan in one of her first design jobs.

Story's path wasn't always leading to a career in decorating. She graduated from the University of San Diego with a degree in psychology but found that work in that field simply made her too sad, as did working in marketing. "I was sitting one day looking at spreadsheets and I thought, 'I don't like this.' So I went back to school for design." The rest, as one might say, is Sara's story.

Above: In the living room, books and treasured objects are arranged on wraparound shelves backed with Farrow & Ball wallpaper. "The patterned wallpaper gave an extra punch to the otherwise neutral colors of the room," says Story. A pair of spoon chairs, a Chesterfield leather sofa, and upholstered chairs by Luther Quintana are positioned on top of a Greek key motif rug from Beauvais carpets. **Left:** A row of Thai statues purchased in Myanmar line the living room fireplace hearth. "I adore exotic travel and finding treasures from far-flung places to bring into my home," says Story.

Left: A small office carved out of a former entryway is covered in Asian-inspired wallpaper from de Gournay.
Below: Story designed a dressing area behind the headboard wall in the master bedroom. The linens are from her line for Casa Del Bianco, and the carpet is from Beauvais.

Above left: The top floor study is a playful mix of furnishings and textiles. "I had been to Morocco prior to designing this space and was inspired by the vibrant colors and focus on craftsmanship," says Story. A suzani is draped across a small sofa covered in silk velvet from Andrew Martin, and a bold geometric rug was purchased in Istanbul. **Above:** Painted black bookcases lined with lively wallpaper by Zoffany display a collection of red lacquer objects from Myanmar. "The wallpaper had an authentic vintage feel that appealed to me," says Story. **Left:** An iron daybed by Jacques Adnet is positioned in the middle of the room. The nearby bar is by Gio Ponti, and the abstract painting, *Karma Punk*, is by Peter Burns. **Opposite:** Crimson-colored wainscoting and floor tile from Marrakesh give the study bath an exotic feel. The sink is from Urban Archaeology, and the fixtures are from Urban Electric.

Q+A
with Sara Story

In a few words, describe your design style.
Timeless, layered, approachable, tailored

What four designers would you like to invite to dinner?
Mies van der Rohe, Louise Bourgeois, Pablo Picasso, and Andrée Putman

Name a past designer, artist, or creative who has had the most influence on your style.
Jacques Adnet and Jean-Michel Frank

What would your perfect room look like?
Casual elegance—a result of layers of textures, a mix of vintage and contemporary furniture, and fantastic pops of color in the art

What are some of the design rules you've had to unlearn as you've become more experienced?
Being freer with experimenting against the norms—mixing high with low to create an eclectic interior

What's your best budget-friendly design hack?
Finding great rugs in Morocco or fabricating a fantastic piece with creative materials for cost savings

What's the simplest and best design rule?
Form follows function—everything has to make sense. Design must work, but it can also be chic and beautiful.

What's a design risk worth taking?
Experimenting with color

Tell us ways that you've used lighting to resolve a dark room.
I find that fantastic layered lighting coupled with fun wall treatments (such as lacquer) can help lighten a dark apartment in an unexpected way.

How do you make your home feel welcoming?
Flowers, cozy fabrics, candles, and of course great music and art!

Where do you go for inspiration?
Traveling. Copenhagen, Milan, Asia—everywhere offers inspiration!

What truly gives a home "life"?
Family and loved ones

How do you solve your storage problems?
Easy. I love to purge. I don't keep a lot of things.

Do you really need all that stuff you have in storage?
I don't have storage!

Any preferences when it comes to your bed linens?
I love them ironed! I have always loved a white bed, but have recently been into whimsical, colorful bedding.

How do you design around your pets?
I actually design with pets in mind! We have a dog whom we love so much—I make sure she has room for her beds, blankets, and toys throughout our home.

What do you covet but can't afford?
The work of some artists I love—John Currin, Ed Ruscha, and Joan Mitchell

What's the best way to start the day?
Meditation, then working out

Long hot soak in the tub or quick shower?
Quick shower

What job would you be terrible at?
Being a politician!

What kind of music do you listen to at home?
I fire up a Spotify playlist—usually Paul Kalkbrenner or Phoenix.

What smells of home for you?
Jasmine or gardenia

What's the first thing you do when you come home from a trip?
Unpack

What's your weekend routine?
Trying to spend as much time in nature!

Do you wish you could spend more time at home?
I already spend a lot of time at home—it's one of my favorite places!

Where is your favorite place to take a nap?
I don't nap too much! But I do love my bedroom—it overlooks the park so the treetops are lovely.

How do you make sure you enjoy your own parties?
I invite an eclectic mix of guests and get everything prepared before people arrive.

How do you subtly let guests know you want them to leave?
I go to bed!

How do you stock a perfect bar?
For me it's four things: tequila, vodka, club soda, and limes!

What's your favorite cocktail?
Good tequila, club soda, and a squeeze of lime

What sorts of things do you like to do the "old-fashioned" way?
Writing thank-you notes (always handwritten) and setting a beautiful table—small gestures that carry traditional details!

What's the best thing about living in New York?
The exposure to art and culture—it puts you in proximity to such creative and bright people.

What's the worst thing about living in New York?
The lack of nature

What do you hope never changes in New York?
The mix of cultures—NYC needs to keep some grit and atmosphere.

What small things make a bad New York day better?
Great friends and a visit to an art gallery or museum always make my days better.

Ronald Bricke

ASSURED ELEGANCE

Above: In the foyer, a photograph by Wang Wusheng, *Celestial Morning*, hangs above a Flemish table displaying a careful arrangement of silver sea urchins, a Roman torso, and a handcrafted ceramic box.

Opposite: A seating area arranged at an angle includes Egyptian Revival chairs, a coffee table by T. H. Robsjohn-Gibbings, and oversize pieces of Gouda pottery.

Ronald Bricke understands the struggles of young designers, and believes they have to deal with much more than he did when he first began his career. "When I started with Yale R. Burge, there was a system. People came for a specific look, and the look we offered was country French," he says. Despite whatever changes the industry has seen, he has successfully adapted to them and has run his own firm since the 1970s.

Bricke graduated from Parsons School of Design where he received a life-changing scholarship that was judged by, somewhat incredibly, the Duchess of Windsor and Salvador Dalí. The award allowed him to realize his dream of studying in Europe for several months. Soon he learned French and bought an apartment in Paris, which he still owns. Decades later, he found a blue velvet box among the items for sale at the Sotheby's auction of the Windsors' possessions. Inside the box lay a photograph of the judging panel, and on the reverse someone had written, "Ronald Bricke was the prize winner."

The box, which he bought, isn't displayed in his Upper East Side apartment, but the same design sensibility that won him the scholarship certainly is. White walls and upholstery allow the eye to engage with a mix of styles and eras. A pre-dynastic Egyptian pottery jar stands beside a ceramic vessel designed by Roy Hamilton, and glass vitrines, originally from a department store in Milan, house sculptural corals. To achieve varied strata, small tables are placed under larger ones, and paintings are occasionally placed below a normal line of sight.

Although Bricke likes "occasional flights of fancy and delight," much of his work is quiet, elegant, and very assured. That said, he is confident when working outside his comfort zone—he was once faced with the challenge of designing a home around a massive collection of colorful art, and when he finished, he somewhat anxiously called the client to hear how they were enjoying the design. "Every night when I go to bed, I pray," the client said, "and you're always included in my prayers because the apartment gives me so much pleasure."

Above: "To create different levels of interest I tuck smaller tables and objects under other tables. It gives me more space to display my collections and attracts the eye to unexpected places," says Bricke. An adorable bronze turtle, once a fountain, peeks out from under a Gae Aulenti coffee table outfitted with a ceramic pumpkin, a Roman torso, and a pair of silver candlesticks. **Left:** Freestanding glass shelving is filled with a mélange of coral, glass, and ceramic sculpture. **Opposite:** Breaking up the all-white backdrop, Bricke covered a fauteuil in velvet with a bold checkered pattern from Clarence House. Nearby, a cipollino marble table displays a brass vase by Gustave Serrurier-Bovy and a ceramic sculpture by Kishi Eiko.

Q+A

with Ronald Bricke

In a few words, describe your design style.
Eclectic, relaxed, modern with traditional

What four designers would you like to invite to dinner?
Axel Vervoordt, Albert Hadley, Elsie de Wolfe, and Carlo Scarpa

What would your perfect room look like?
Sunlit and comfortable, with Greek sculpture, soft and firm seating, and intriguing accessories

What are some of the design rules you've had to unlearn as you've become more experienced?
Don't just listen to a client. Interpret what you think will make them happy.

What's your best budget-friendly design hack?
Paint

What's a design risk worth taking?
If you think it will improve the lives of you or your client, do it!

Tell us ways that you've used lighting to resolve a dark room.
Hidden LEDs—behind or under furniture, pedestals, or objects. Use fewer lamps and no recessed lights.

Where do you go for inspiration?
The outside world

What truly gives a home "life"?
Having friends enjoy it with you

How do you solve your storage problems?
I can't. I'm always buying and filling up any storage I have.

Do you really need all that stuff you have in storage?
No, but I love the ability to change things frequently in my apartment.

Any preferences when it comes to your bed linens?
They must be real linen—fresh, pressed, and white.

What do you covet but can't afford?
A house by Ricardo Legorreta

What's the best way to start the day?
A shower, a good cappuccino, and a newspaper

What job would you be terrible at?
Fabricating any of the designs I create

What kind of music do you listen to at home?
Classical

What smells of home for you?
Good food being cooked and Asiatic lilies

What's the first thing you do when you come home from a trip?
Unpack and buy flowers

What's your weekend routine?
Drive to the country, wander by the creek, walk the paths in the garden, visit the local organic farm, eat a great breakfast, get together with friends, buy vegetables for the week

Do you wish you could spend more time at home?
Definitely, during the day. I would get my reading done, and it would be like reading on the island of Santorini.

How long can you go without tidying up?
At most a couple of hours

Where is your favorite place to take a nap?
My Corbu [Le Corbusier] chaise

How do you make sure you enjoy your own parties?
By inviting interesting people. I love to learn.

How do you subtly let guests know you want them to leave?
"Let's move to the other room. It's more comfortable."

How do you stock a perfect bar?
Lots of champagne and fine wine, Izarra, good Scotch, and gin for my 92-year-old lady friend

What sorts of things do you like to do the "old-fashioned" way?
Almost every night I sit at the table with good china, good silverware, candles, flowers, and wonderful home-cooked food.

What's the best thing about living in New York?
Access to incredible resources and the Q train

What's the worst thing about living in New York?
Traffic

What do you hope never changes in New York?
The vitality

How do you get around town?
Lyft, Uber, Q train, or on foot

Is there a particular place in the city that has a special meaning for you?
The former restaurant with the pool at the Metropolitan Museum of Art

Bricke enveloped the master bedroom in white curtains that can be opened or closed to reveal different groupings of art displayed on the walls.

Stephen Sills

REFINEMENT AND TEXTURE

"I always had a singular vision of what I wanted to do," says Stephen Sills. "I was like a self-induced adult at the age of fifteen. I wasn't interested in what other kids were doing. I wanted to be an artist." Sills most definitely is an original. Few designers have his ability to compose a room by synthesizing the refined and the exquisite with the rough-hewn, hand-finished surfaces that inspire him—he loves building materials such as cement, marble, and plaster.

"You have to *feel* the material," he says. Tactility, the touch of the hand both in the making and the experience of the finishes, is key. Hand-scored plaster, burnished metals, and stone floors are some of his signature markers, as is tone-on-tone monochromatic color with what he calls an "off-color" to energize the whole.

Sills is unafraid to introduce an element of the strange as well: in his Bedford Hills, New York, home, he uses what he describes as "pond-scum green" for one of the guest bedrooms. His study has a sculpture of an eagle's nest in tangled barbed wire, which speaks directly to an intricately stitched, antique Portuguese embroidery in silver thread that is draped over the back of a sofa. Furniture has patina and fluid line, and upholstery is simple. There is a luminous, even mysterious purity to his work, which is never over decorated and always closely considered. Perhaps this luminosity is a reflection of the wide sky that surrounds Durant, Oklahoma, where he grew up, which he says still influences him.

Graduating with a degree in interior design from the University of North Texas, Sills spent three years in Paris, and after a short period working as a designer in Dallas he found his way to New York, where he met James Huniford. Soon afterward they founded Sills Huniford, which became one of the most influential design firms in the city.

Now working alone, Sills doesn't see himself as a perfectionist so much as someone who is always changing things. He is simply at his happiest when he is actually "doing."

The living room's hand-scored plaster walls and stone floors are the perfect backdrop for Sills's mix of fine art and antiques.

Above: In the main entrance hall, Sills used felt-tip markers to hand color the stripes of the Italian silk velvet that covers the Jacobean chairs, once owned by Billy Baldwin. Marble columns from the Mamluk period frame the view to the living room. **Above right:** "The most important thing is to live with things you love, whether they are from a top Paris gallery or a flea market," says Sills. To hide the disparate patterns of book spines in the library he lined the glass-fronted bookcases with inexpensive bamboo shades and painted them white. **Right:** A Robert Rauschenberg drawing and a Louis XVI settee are centered between the French doors in the front of the living room. Sills references the property's many trees with a small eighteenth-century English twig stand.

Above: Christian Dior once owned the eighteenth-century porter's chair that stands front and center in Sills's library.
Right: In the dining room, a chandelier by Alberto Giacometti and French Directoire sconces illuminate a painting by Joan Miró. Sills hand-stained and lacquered the gourds to create a distinctive centerpiece.

Above left: Sills chose soft, calming colors and spare furnishings for the master bedroom. **Left:** A tufted leather sofa and mahogany Directoire chair provide elegant and comfortable seating in a corner of the guest bedroom.

Above: Sills converted a dilapidated garage with a tree growing through it into a guesthouse. "So many friends have stayed here, but I often use it for myself. It's a perfect combination of summerhouse and artist's studio," says Sills. The walls were plastered in two shades of tinted white, and the Canadian marble-brick floors are further stained, also in a white. The designer placed eighteenth-century English grotto tables among Louis XVI chairs and a gilt Regency sofa.

Q+A
with Stephen Sills

In a few words, describe your design style.
Classic, original elegance with a European bent

What four designers would you like to invite to dinner?
Henri Samuel, Billy Baldwin, Jean-Michel Frank, and Frances Elkins

What would your perfect room look like?
Great proportions, great light, and for it to be by the sea or in a garden

What are some of the design rules you've had to unlearn as you've become more experienced?
Putting confidence in your clients

What's your best budget-friendly design hack?
An IKEA kitchen—affordable and great looking

What's the simplest and best design rule?
Good housekeeping

What's a design risk worth taking?
Color

Where do you go for inspiration?
Everywhere on the planet and in your own backyard

Tell us ways that you've used lighting to resolve a dark room.
Uplights

How do you make your home feel welcoming?
Comfort and fires—or plants

What truly gives a home "life"?
People and plants

How do you solve your storage problems?
Basements and barns

Do you really need all that stuff you have in storage?
No

Any preferences when it comes to your bed linens?
Just to use good cotton

How do you design around your pets?
Dog cookies in a large industrial jar in the kitchen

What do you covet but can't afford?
Nothing

What have you broken that you still mourn?
A large, broken Roman glass

What's the best way to start the day?
Make your own bed

Long hot soak in the tub or quick shower?
A quick shower, but also an occasional tub soak

What job would you be terrible at?
Accounting

What kind of music do you listen to at home?
Classical, Beethoven

What smells of home for you?
The scent of the garden, fresh-cut grass,
and fireplaces

**What's the first thing you do when you come
home from a trip?**
Unpack my clothes

What's your weekend routine?
Working in the gardens and, in the winter,
making fires

Do you wish you could spend more time at home?
Yes

How long can you go without tidying up?
Not less than five minutes

Where is your favorite place to take a nap?
My bed

**How do you make sure you enjoy your own
parties?**
Have help

**How do you subtly let guests know you want
them to leave?**
Grow weary of the conversation . . . or get out of
my chair.

How do you stock a perfect bar?
To have all hard liquors available and all mixers—
presented in their original bottles (as long as they're
attractive)

What's your favorite cocktail?
Dry gin martini

**What sorts of things do you like to do the
"old-fashioned" way?**
Design boards for presentations

What's the best thing about living in New York?
For me, the variations of museum collections and the
energy and diversity of the people that live here

What's the worst thing about living in New York?
The winters

What do you hope never changes in New York?
Creativity

How do you get around town?
Subway, taxi, Uber, and private cars

**Is there a particular place in the city that has a
special meaning for you?**
The Metropolitan Museum of Art

Ellie Cullman

ARTISANAL CHARM

Above: In a corner of the foyer, Adolph Gottlieb's *Iconic Burst* (1973) hangs above an 1815 American center table. **Opposite:** Cullman was so taken with the Persian blue, apricot, and cinnamon colors of an antique Tabriz rug that she planned the rest of the library around it. Kenneth Noland's *Warm Reverie* (1962) adds a touch of modernity to the space and continues the vibrant hues of the rug.

Ellie Cullman graduated Phi Beta Kappa magna cum laude from Barnard College. It firmly says so in the first line of her official biography, and it's hard to imagine she would have graduated with anything else.

She laughs at her own perfectionism ("OMG, I'm so type A!"), but her meticulous attention to high-end detail was key in turning her into one of the real "couture" designers. Obsessed with artisanal excellence, exemplified in her own home by painted surfaces overlaid with glazes, waxes, and gilding, as well as by the Lesage silk embroidery on the curtains precisely placed so that no detail is lost in the folds, she says she could write a whole book about trim alone. "It's the little subtle things—I think that's what's most important about design."

Every project, Cullman declares, must start with her falling in love with something, be it a paint color, a piece of furniture, or a particular aesthetic. Without love, there can't be that true passion necessary to enliven the essential elements of design: scale, order, and function. Cullman began a PhD in Japanese at Columbia University, worked at Japan Society, and spent two years living in Japan in the 1970s, and her love of that aesthetic is expressed in almost all of the fourteen rooms of her Park Avenue duplex, which she shares with her husband, Edgar. In the living room, a six-panel eighteenth-century screen depicting Kyoto instantly draws the eye, and other screens are equally impressive: these include a particularly magical green-and-gold nineteenth-century panel of floating fans, which graces the bedroom. The real showstopper, the hand-painted wallpaper in the dining room showing scenes of village life, is Chinese.

And then there is the very American candy—bowls of bright jellybeans and foil-covered chocolates are dotted here and there. Along with abundant fresh flowers, it's a typical grace note. Cullman, who was raised in Brooklyn and whose family owns the famed Peter Luger Steak House, grew up with bowls of candy in her childhood home. "I like having candy in a room. It makes me happy."

In addition to having three grown children—Trip, a theater director; Sam, a filmmaker; and Georgina, an environmental scientist—Cullman has also had other careers, including working as a curator at the American Folk Art Museum. This is yet another aesthetic that informs her eye.

Left: In the living room, Venetian plaster in a rich terra-cotta color with a gold wash is illuminated by an Austrian gilt chandelier. A shimmering Japanese six-panel screen depicting a view of Kyoto contrasts with English Regency armchairs covered in a dashing leopard-print velvet. **Below left:** Cullman lightened the formality of the living room by injecting such modern elements as *The Green One* (1972) by Adolph Gottlieb and the toned-down, hand-embroidered curtains by Lesage. **Below:** Fresh flowers and bowls of candy throughout the living room give the space a welcoming atmosphere.

Opposite: Cullman hosts dinner parties in her handsomely furnished dining room, which showcases walls covered in an extraordinary hand-painted Chinese wallpaper dated around 1770. An impressive Louis XVI–style gilt bronze-and-crystal chandelier is suspended from a gold-glazed ceiling.

Right: The walls of the stairwell are filled with a large sampling of works on paper from a variety of American artists, including Robert Henri, John Marin, Yasuo Kuniyoshi, and Maurice Prendergast. **Below:** A rare sandstone sixth- or seventh-century male divinity from India keeps watch over the double height foyer. Cullman offset the richness of the faux-marquetry painted floors by covering the walls in squares of cream-colored parchment paper.

Above: The master bedroom is all about comfort. A custom bed from Charles H. Beckley is outfitted in linens from E. Braun & Co. On the far wall, *Fruit Vendors* (c. 1899) by Everett Shinn hangs above a neoclassical Italian 1870s walnut-and-fruitwood commode. **Above right:** In the master bathroom, a pair of vanities is topped with slabs of Calacatta marble. **Right:** Cullman's dressing room was once one of the children's bedrooms. Now it is outfitted with walls and doors painted in celadon green with gilt highlights and delicate eglomise panels.

Q+A

with Ellie Cullman

In a few words, describe your design style.
Modern traditional. While the DNA of my company is rooted in traditional design and a passion for antiques, we are also embracing modernism with great enthusiasm. There is nothing more exciting than the alchemy that happens when old meets new and when new meets old.

Name a past designer, artist, or creative who has had the most influence on your style.
Albert Hadley and Mark Hampton. While Albert's approach derived from modernism, Mark's was deeply rooted in classicism and traditionalism. These two titans were able to do absolutely anything, skillfully navigating the waters between traditional and modern.

What's your best budget-friendly design hack?
1) Paint! A fresh coat of paint really makes a space feel renewed and is a cost-effective way to make a major difference. 2) Lampshades! Change your lampshades—especially if you have a dark green or black one in a room that needs more light. If you change all of your shades to uniform off-white linen, you will notice an immediate, uplifting effect.
3) There is also nothing more cathartic for me than

to re-do every bookshelf and tabletop—I call it "apartment therapy." Tabletops, like bookcases, must be arranged and organized with thought. Start by taking everything down, and then carefully put it back, looking at each shelf and every surface as if for the first time. Keep in mind that every tabletop deserves the same considerations as the floor plan of a room to create a cosmos of form, material, and color.

What's the simplest and best design rule?
Form and function are the twin pillars of interior design, and there is a delicate balance between the two. Regarding function: Is there a seating arrangement that allows for conversation? Is there a table to put a drink on? Is there a lamp by which to read? Regarding form: Is the architecture in sympathy with the decoration? Is there equilibrium between hard and soft furnishings, lighting, art, and antiques? It is never enough to have just a beautiful interior—it must function as well.

Tell us ways that you've used lighting to resolve a dark room.
While plenty of modern-day architecture has design flaws, the biggest one for us is poor lighting. Many developers take the easy way out and pepper the

ceiling with a grid of down lights, which cast a dark shadow on the ceiling and light our faces in an unflattering way. Instead, we are obsessed with layered lighting, which creates pools of flattering light for even and interesting illumination. Layered lighting is best achieved by using more than one light source and a mixture of lighting types, including ceiling lights, wall lights, and lamps.

Where do you go for inspiration?
Travel is endlessly inspiring. I spent two years in Japan, which were pivotal to the development of my design aesthetic, but I have found that inspiration is everywhere: the russet red in a Rothko painting, the patterned floor of Piazza San Marco in Venice. Everything your eye sees is a catalyst for a color, motif, or pattern that can be incorporated into an interior. Also, the women in my office endlessly inspire me. They have pushed our firm past the comfort zone of primarily working with antiques to embracing cutting-edge design.

What truly gives a home "life"?
The personal collections and memorabilia of the owner

What smells of home for you?
A roast chicken in the oven

What's the first thing you do when you come home from a trip?
Go straight to the hairdresser.

Do you have a treasured piece of clothing in your closet?
Oh I can't say it's one piece of clothing, I have an extensive wardrobe of leopard prints. After all, leopard is classic; it never goes out of style.

How do you make sure you enjoy your own parties?
By getting someone to cook for me. When I was younger, I cooked a lot and went through Julia Child and Craig Claiborne cover to cover. I also weighed ten pounds more!

What's your favorite cocktail?
Dry gin martini on ice (unlike James Bond, I like it stirred not shaken) with a twist of lemon peel

What sorts of things do you like to do the "old-fashioned" way?
I still read everything in print—books, magazines, and the paper. It's just not the same on a Kindle or a computer.

What's the best thing about living in New York?
The smorgasbord of activities available—from film, theater, classical music, jazz, and rock to an endless explosion of new restaurants

What's the worst thing about living in New York?
It's difficult to find a quiet place.

What do you hope never changes in New York?
The different ethnic neighborhoods all over the city. What a rich tapestry we live in!

Cullman grew up with bowls of candy throughout her childhood home and continues the practice today: "It makes me happy."

Samuel Botero

ART AND WHIMSY

In 1962, at the age of thirteen, Colombian-born Samuel Botero arrived in New York. Since then, he has been so smitten with the city that he has written, "I know that I would have become less than what I am without New York." Perhaps, but it's more than likely his design talent would have flourished in any city, and it's now certainly showcased in rooms across the world. Intuitive and in love with color, Botero pays no particular attention to rules and creates spaces full of warmth, flair, and, most notably, imagination—all qualities that can be found in his Upper East Side apartment. His imagination was evident as a child, when the nuns at his Catholic school in Bogotá would punish him for doodling endlessly instead of paying attention to schoolwork. It turns out he was struggling with dyslexia, which was only diagnosed in his thirties. Dyslexia affects him every day, and he wryly notes the irony of being in a profession where wrong measurements make for expensive mistakes.

Despite this, he is not one who is easily defeated. When he was seven, he sent a letter to the president of Colombia because he believed that somewhere in his office was a machine that could print money. If he could just be president for five minutes, Botero thought, he could help his struggling single mother. The newspapers recorded the visit with photographs of little Botero dwarfed by the president's imposing desk. What the story reveals, Botero feels, is how he is comfortable with anyone. What he also learned, he adds, is that "if you want something, go straight to the top."

After winning a scholarship to Pratt Institute, he worked as a design intern, a model, and an illustrator for a shoe catalog. Eventually, he got two big breaks: first, he designed a house in Mexico for the fashion designer Ken Scott where everything was "green on green on green." Then, he designed Princess Yasmin Aga Khan's Manhattan apartment in the San Remo. When that apartment was featured in *Architectural Digest*, Botero had arrived. He is now a regular on the AD100 list. "I like being a star," he says with soft-spoken frankness. "It's what I always wanted to be."

A pair of Danish Art Deco chairs, covered in a gaufrage velvet, is a lively juxtaposition to a nineteenth-century gilt papier-mâché side chair and a Danish chair covered in a blue-and-dull-gold Fortuny fabric. The cobalt Chinese Art Deco rug works as a foil to all the reds, pinks, and golds.

Above: In the living room, a colorful Hunt Slonem painting hangs above an Art Deco credenza that is covered in cream leather and illuminated by a pair of Billy Haines carved-wood lamps.

Above: In the study, Botero installed art and masks salon style, enabling him to display more of his extensive collection. "I find it necessary to be surrounded by art. It inspires me every day," says the designer. **Left:** Deep brown walls, an olive-green ceiling, and fuchsia curtains and trim are a dramatic backdrop for both the artwork and the mix of furniture. Botero believes in being patient and decorating over time: "We live in an age of instant coffee and instant gratification."

Left and below: Botero and his husband, Emery, are particularly drawn to Asian art. The master bedroom is lined with a framed twelve-panel watercolor series of a Japanese poem. A Samurai screen from the Edo period hangs above an Italian Art Deco bed. Three Sharaku wood blocks complete the wall composition.

Q+A

with Samuel Botero

In a few words, describe your design style.
I respond to the client's personality and style, interpreting those traits into a design vocabulary for them. Not everyone is the same. Color is an essential part of my style. I have never attracted beige people.

What four designers would you like to invite to dinner?
Ben Baldwin, my mentor; Renzo Mongiardino, whose sense of fantasy and illusion is timeless; Robert Couturier, whose classic and easy elegance is beautifully conceived; and Zaha Hadid, who insinuated the female curve into the angular world of male architects.

What would your perfect room look like?
To me, a room I live in must combine elegance, comfort, and the unexpected with a dash of humor.

What are some of the design rules you've had to unlearn as you've become more experienced?
I have stopped following trends and look at rules with a jaundiced eye. There are few rules that are irrevocable, except the law of gravity.

What's the simplest and best design rule?

Don't force anything, no matter how much you like it. If it doesn't flow, it won't work.

Tell us ways that you've used lighting to resolve a dark room.
A dark room is an opportunity to create drama. We use color from a medium to a saturated palette. We add dimension by using multiple light sources such as small table lamps or directed lights on objects or works of art with ceiling spots. This creates a chiaroscuro effect, making a dark room sexy and interesting and enlarging the space. It is also a very flattering light for people. Never paint a dark space white. It will just look dingy.

How do you make your home feel welcoming?
A seating plan that's inviting and accessible. Details like handy surfaces for drinks, cloth hand towels in the powder room in a basket, flowers in small vases placed about for color and beauty, and a consideration for personal needs. Flattering lighting that has warmth (no LED). Beautiful objects to draw the eye. A pleasant and subtle fragrance from a candle, never cloying or sweet.

Where do you go for inspiration?

My memories, my library, museums, daydreams, music, Internet wanderings. Anything that opens the mind.

What truly gives a home "life"?
Things that mean something to you. Items picked up on trips, gifts from friends (with good taste). Objects are memory signposts. Without these intimate items, there is no past, so no "life."

How do you solve your storage problems?
A designer's curse, rented storage, which we're now trying to get rid of. Avoid the black hole of storage.

Do you really need all that stuff you have in storage?
A life lesson I should have learned years ago: If you don't miss it, you don't need it.

What have you broken that you still mourn?
Things pass. You honor them for a moment, then move on. There is no joy in regret.

What do you covet but can't afford?
Private air travel all the time, not just with clients

What kind of music do you listen to at home?
Standards of the Great American Songbook. Latin music of most genres. Classical, especially Mozart, Bach, and Saint-Saëns. Buddha Bar.

What smells of home for you?
Fortuny candles, which are wonderful, and coffee

How do you make sure you enjoy your own parties?
Hire caterers, invite a mix of people who you would not normally put together, relax, and let it unfold.

How do you subtly let guests know you want them to leave?
I tell them about a line from a Three Stooges short I loved as a child: "Come back when you can't stay so long." It usually works without harm or insult and leaves them laughing.

How do you stock a perfect bar?
With consideration for all the basic drinks that people like. Beautiful glasses and accessories. The ritual of the cocktail is like a tea ceremony and should be special and festive.

What's your favorite cocktail?
Boring as it is, my favorite is a white-wine spritzer with lots of ice as the Europeans do, preferably in a beautiful tall Venini glass.

What sorts of things do you like to do the "old-fashioned" way?
I like to shop in person whenever possible, unless I already know the product. The Internet doesn't tell you quality or true color and texture. I must see and touch.

What's the best thing about living in New York?
The access to just about anything your heart desires

What's the worst thing about living in New York?
Confronting just about everything your heart doesn't desire

What do you hope never changes in New York?
The variety of people who can still live in the city. Homogeneity is a bore.

What small things make a bad New York day better?
A walk through Central Park, a stroll through a museum, or meeting friends for a drink

How do you get around town?
Cab or Uber. Sometimes the subway for a long jaunt or during bad traffic.

Is there a particular place in the city that has a special meaning for you?
The Cloisters. It's a sanctuary I love, especially when I need to cleanse my mind. It goes back to my college days.

Vicente Wolf

A COOL SERENITY

Above: In the living area, a large surrealist painting, *Men Carry Mattress through the Desert* by Australian artist Graeme Drendel, is positioned above a 1940s chest from France. **Opposite:** In the media room and guest bedroom, a large photograph of trees taken by Wolf hangs above a custom iron daybed.

For someone who is something of a rebel, Vicente Wolf has a design aesthetic that is, interestingly, always serene.

Wolf came to New York from Cuba when he was eighteen, having never graduated from high school, and began modeling, taking acting classes, and "sweeping floors." He tried design school, but walked out when an instructor insisted that curtains were supposed to hang two inches above the floor. Although shy and reticent to talk about himself, he has strong opinions and is passionate about his work; he describes himself as having a Latino interior covered in a shell of New York sophistication.

Wolf's Garment District loft is as tranquil as the numerous projects he has completed all over the world. One of his greatest pleasures is seeing the light from his windows create patterns on the floor, illustrating his appreciation for subtle change and the nuances of color. He prefers to prop photographs from his collection of more than six hundred mostly vintage works on shelves, so they can be viewed from different angles and because he likes the freedom to move them around. "When something hangs in one place for too long, you stop seeing it," he explains.

An accomplished photographer himself, Wolf has traveled around the world and has a particular love for Papua New Guinea, Indonesia, and Borneo. His hallmark white is used throughout the loft because he finds the hue "very architectural" and it provides the perfect backdrop for pieces brought back from his many trips. To avoid too many formal lines in a square space, furniture is randomly placed around and tends to be curved and textured. It's a wonderful play of contrasts, the product of a deeply instinctive approach.

"I'm self-taught in everything I do. I'm dyslexic, so the format of learning in school did not work for me. What you see here is what I can see in my mind before it's created."

Right: White concrete floors and plaster walls are the perfect setting for Wolf's extensive collection of art and photography. Simple wall ledges and a row of mismatched vintage chairs enable Wolf to rotate the installation at whim.
Below: A mixture of furniture placed at an angle seems to float within the light-filled, open-floor living space. A large Buddha statue stands near an eighteenth-century French gilt bench anda tribal chair from Ethiopia. "The space called for unconventional arrangements, and I like that," says Wolf.

Right: A peek into the master bathroom from Wolf's bedroom. A nineteenth-century Chinese chair stands at the entrance. **Below:** A table from Burma was converted into a washstand. A frosted-glass wall, which is the back of the bookcase in the library, allows light into the bathroom. **Below right:** A forklift is ingeniously used as a television stand in the master bedroom.

Above: Floor-to-ceiling wool curtains give a sense of grandeur to the ten-foot-high ceilings in Wolf's bedroom. "I wake up at five-thirty every morning, so they are perfect for shielding early morning light," says Wolf. A headboard covered in fabric from Wolf's VW Home line stands in front of an angled freestanding wall that is used for storage. **Right:** Objects collected from world travels—including prayer beads, silver bracelets, and vintage toy cars—are on display throughout the loft.

Q+A

with Vicente Wolf

In a few words, describe your design style.
Clean, comfortable, timeless, and modern

What four designers would you like to invite to dinner?
Billy Baldwin, El Anatsui, Mies van der Rohe, and Stephen Sondheim

What would your perfect room look like?
A square space full of light, with a ceiling no higher than twelve feet, very large windows, and a magnificent view

What are some of the design rules you've had to unlearn as you've become more experienced?
I didn't go to design school, so all the rules I have are the ones I made up myself.

What's your best budget-friendly design hack?
Chaises from Crate & Barrel

What's the simplest and best design rule?
Less is more

What's a design risk worth taking?
Stepping out of your comfort zone. It's important to take risks to grow as a creative person.

Tell us ways that you've used lighting to resolve a dark room.
You need to have three types of lighting. Overhead for general illumination, uplighting for drama, and lamps to give the room warmth and intimacy.

How do you make your home feel welcoming?
I make sure it smells good and has a relaxed feeling to it. It's important to make guests feel at home, whether they're helping themselves to food in the refrigerator or simply reading a book in the living room.

Where do you go for inspiration?
I travel. The more primitive, the less like New York— the more inspiration I get.

What truly gives a home "life"?
Your soul, not possessions or the superficial things in life

How do you solve your storage problems?
I use a lot of baskets and shelves, so everything is accessible.

Any preferences when it comes to your bed linens?

I buy linens all over the world, but they must be all cotton and pressed. I change my bed linens three times a week.

How do you design around your pets?
I don't design specifically around my cat, but I am starting to use more and more indoor-outdoor fabrics that are completely washable.

What's the best way to start the day?
Exercising, meditating, and putting a smile on your face

What kind of music do you listen to at home?
I love Brazilian music and classics like Sinatra and Garland. Anything but country western.

What smells of home for you?
Fresh flowers and the ocean

What's the first thing you do when you come home from a trip?
Unpack. Sort and do my laundry, then put everything away.

What's your weekend routine?
I get up at 5:30, believe it or not, go running, and make coffee. Then I go into town (Montauk) and have breakfast at the Latino shop. Then I spend time in my garden until around 3:00, then shower and relax and get ready to go out for dinner.

How long can you go without tidying up?
I don't mind letting things go a bit; a perfect space is off-putting. But I do always make my bed first thing in the morning.

How do you make sure you enjoy your own parties?
It's important to prepare in advance—make sure you have the right mix of people, serve great food and liquor, then just let go of control and enjoy the evening.

How do you stock a perfect bar?
It's important to have a good selection of glassware, champagne flutes, highballs, wine glasses, a beautiful ice bucket, and utensils

What's your favorite cocktail?
I don't drink cocktails. It would have to be straight vodka or tequila.

What sorts of things do you like to do the "old-fashioned" way?
I read magazines and the *New York Times* paper edition every morning. I also use a broom to clean my floors, and I do my own gardening. And I much prefer the telephone to texting.

What's the best thing about living in New York?
Choices

What do you hope never changes in New York?
This is an oxymoron question, as New York is all about change whether you like it or not.

Misha, Wolf's adored cat, ensconced on an antique Chinese chair

Amanda Nisbet

A PASSION FOR COLOR

Amanda Nisbet didn't originally want to be a designer—she wanted to be an actress. "But I had very little patience," she says. "My name wasn't instantly in the lights, and I got very frustrated. Meanwhile, people kept asking me, 'Will you do my house? I love your apartment.'" Once she made the decision to focus on design, things came together. "People respected me and trusted me. That's what it's all about."

A keen rider, Nisbet opted for an equestrian boarding school near Washington, DC, whose headmistress, Jean Harris, murdered her lover, the physician who invented the Scarsdale diet. "She was there during my sophomore year," Nisbet recalls. "It was right out of a novel!" Nisbet survived the drama and went on to study art history, and then worked for a number of years at Christie's. Her own design firm was founded in 1998, and it was not long before her name was on the A-list.

"I'm not necessarily confident in all areas of my life, but I'm confident in this," Nisbet declares. And rightly so. Known for her livable and lively designs, she deftly uses fresh color to lend energy to a room. There isn't a single color that she dislikes, and she often starts the process by spreading a bunch of colored fabrics on the floor to see how they will direct the design. Her own home in Carnegie Hill is full of jewel tones, with a softer palette used in the bedrooms. She attributes her love of color partially to her Canadian upbringing; she is originally from Montreal. "Because of the cold winters, I like to make things cozy—even if I'm decorating in Palm Beach." Without any formal training, Nisbet doesn't really follow the rules—a process that she finds liberating. "I think you have to have innate style," she says matter-of-factly, "and the rest isn't rocket science."

In her living room, Nisbet employs shades of violet, raspberry, and tangerine and mixes them with lush textures, heirloom furniture, and interesting objects: punchy orange boiled-wool curtains, raised to ceiling height; purple cushions that top Lucite stools; a handmade mirror by Eve Kaplan and a gilt French console, both from Gerald Bland.

Left: In the study, fabrics and furniture are given a jolt of energy with lacquered walls in Jalapeño Pepper from Benjamin Moore. "I just love how paint color gives a pop to everything in the room," says Nisbet. **Below left:** In the dining room, Nisbet modernized traditional tufted chairs by applying black lacquer to the legs and upholstering them in a brown-and-white ikat fabric from Madeline Weinrib. Blue Wedgwood urns stand beneath a gilt mirror, another family heirloom. **Below:** Lilac silk-covered chairs are given definition with gold-colored trim. Paintings and a mirror hang on Venetian plaster walls.

Below: The light-filled master bedroom has an ethereal feeling, highlighted by pale colors and artwork. "I believe in a soft palette for the bedroom," says Nisbet. *Maura River Cliffs* by Ray Kass hangs on a wall painted in Farrow & Ball's Tallow. A pair of chairs by Barbara Barry adds a touch of Hollywood Regency glamour. A Lucite table stands atop the cream wall-to-wall carpet and is the perfect height to display a pair of terra-cotta busts and magazines.
Left: Nisbet added a feminine, light feeling to the master bathroom by papering the walls in a pink-and-white wallpaper with an exotic pattern from Manuel Canovas.

Q+A

with Amanda Nisbet

In a few words, describe your design style.
Bold, witty, comfortable, COLORFUL

What are some of the design rules you've had to unlearn as you've become more experienced?
I'm not a rule keeper by nature, and if I try to revert to the rules, I don't do my best work.

What's the simplest and best design rule?
"Do you love it?!" That is all that matters.

What's a design risk worth taking?
There aren't many design risks that aren't worth taking! I feel that way about life in general.

Tell us ways that you've used lighting to resolve a dark room.
I use various layers of lighting: table lights, standing lamps, uplights. I always have candles burning and lots of soft, sumptuous throws everywhere.

How do you make your home feel welcoming?
A roaring wood fire would be my preference 365 days of the year. Nothing beats the smell and crackle.

Where do you go for inspiration?
The windows of Bergdorf's and travel, travel, travel

What truly gives a home "life"?
Personal trinkets and family photos

How do you solve your storage problems?
Great question—it's an issue!

Do you really need all that stuff you have in storage?
Yes! You never know what will come back in style.

Any preferences when it comes to your bed linens?
They have to be ironed.

What do you covet but can't afford?
A villa in Italy

What's the best way to start the day?
I really want to start meditating, but I typically have a jug of coffee and hit the ground running.

Long hot soak in the tub or quick shower?
Quick shower—I never seem to indulge in baths but they are fabulous when I do . . . especially during the winter.

What kind of music do you listen to at home?

Tom Petty, Fleetwood Mac, and Beyoncé

What smells of home for you?
Casablanca lilies in abundance

Do you wish you could spend more time at home?
Always! I love being home. With my busy travel schedule, it isn't often I'm home more than a few days. My home is both relaxing and reinvigorating.

How long can you go without tidying up?
Five minutes

Where is your favorite place to take a nap?
My living room sofa wrapped in a cashmere throw

How do you make sure you enjoy your own parties?
I've pre-done all the work. The mood is set. Drinks are chilling, the music is playing, the candles are flickering—all in advance of my guests arriving so I have a minute to sip my tequila and get ready to have fun.

How do you subtly let guests know you want them to leave?
I get in bed—ha! No, typically my party guests leave before I'm ready to turn in for the evening so it's rarely an issue!

How do you stock a perfect bar?
A few top-shelf bottles and lots of fresh ingredients to mix in

What's your favorite cocktail?
Tequila on the rocks with lime

What's the best thing about living in New York?
CHOICES . . . and the speed to which things get done!

What's the worst thing about living in New York?
Traffic

What sorts of things do you like to do the "old-fashioned" way?
Handwritten notes, a phone call (instead of a text!) . . . old-fashioned communication

What do you hope never changes in New York?
Small, unique boutique design shops . . . they are already dwindling!

What small things make a bad New York day better?
A Sant Ambroeus cappuccino with a friend and a quick manicure

How do you get around town?
Walk—that's one of the best parts of being in the city.

Is there a particular place in the city that has a special meaning for you?
Carnegie Hill—it is where I raised my children.

Nisbet decided to wallpaper the ceiling of her son's bedroom in a subtle geometric paper then gave the room a shot of color with a bright red ceiling fixture and headboard.

Alex Papachristidis

MODERN VINTAGE

Above: With its striped walls and ceiling as well as a double-sided bookcase, the entrance hall exudes a sense of warmth and welcome. **Opposite:** Papachristidis combined six different fabrics to create this bold den sofa. The coffee table with a faux Delft-tile top is from John Rosselli Antiques.

When Alex Papachristidis and his partner, Scott Nelson, order pizza, it's swiftly removed from its greasy box and served on the best china. Porcelain, crystal, antique silverware: to Papachristidis, an aesthete to the soles of his bespoke shoes, these are a source of delight in the modern, utilitarian world. He has made certain accommodations with the present moment and is especially fond of Instagram—his profile is @alexsviewpoint—but his apartment in the East 60s definitely has an Old World, European feel.

There is nothing ugly in any of the rooms. His love for beautiful things, he says, has always been with him, in part thanks to his mother, an "Auntie Mame" figure who loved decorating and shopping. It was a relief when she suggested that he leave Skidmore College and go to Parsons School of Design to study interior design. He took on his first project, a large Manhattan apartment, while still a student, and went on to establish his own firm in 1987.

Having been in the business for over three decades, he has learned not to dismiss any particular era or style. So many things have grown on him, he explains, such as an increased appreciation of the Japanese aesthetic and a newfound interest in Arts and Crafts furniture. Characteristically, he upholstered some Arts and Crafts chairs in Fortuny fabric, giving them a whole new life. William Morris might be turning in his grave—or maybe not. There is a spirited originality to this idea, and the chairs complement the meticulously designed rooms in the apartment.

Papachristidis firmly believes that not only his own style is alive and kicking but also another version of it, which he calls "modern vintage," has also been established by a younger generation of designers. These designers, however, can't yet match his "*twenty-seven years* of buying and shopping *competitively*." It's exactly the right time to buy the kinds of furniture and decorative objects that fill his home, he affirms. There are bargains everywhere, especially at auction, because, happily, "all the rich people are into artwork."

He obviously takes much pleasure in his thoughtful, eclectic surroundings. "My partner, Scott, once said to me, 'Why don't we live in a white box?' And I said, 'Because we can't.'"

Left, below, and right: Chinoiserie wallpaper based on an eighteenth-century document that Papachristidis saved for many years and a hand-stenciled parquet de Versailles floor give the living room an elegant old-world feel. "This type of decorating," he says, "is all about history." A plum-colored velvet sofa fits perfectly into a corner of the room. The gilt French armchairs have Claremont geometric-patterned cushions and antique ikat backs. Papachristidis layers richly saturated color and pattern throughout the apartment.

Right: The dining room is a luscious mix of different shades of plum, with wool-felt walls and silk curtains. Fortuny fabric covers chalky-white French chairs, and a nineteenth-century tole chandelier hangs above a custom lacquer table covered with art and design books.

Below: Tree of Life fabric from Manuel Canovas covers the walls and daybed in the office and dressing room of Papachristidis's partner, Scott Nelson. "I wanted to create an old-fashioned gentleman's dressing room and personal haven for Scott," says the designer.

Right: More is more in the master bedroom. An array of artworks is displayed on a Swedish wallpaper from Old World Weavers that reminds Papachristidis of the oval hall at Charles de Beistegui's Château de Groussay.
Below: A 1950s French sunburst mirror is centered above the custom bed, which has a velvet-upholstered headboard, green cut-velvet pillows, and a cotton quilt from Les Indiennes.
Below right: The dapper dresser: Papachristidis's dressing room is never a mess.

Q+A
with Alex Papachristidis

In a few words, describe your design style.
Classic interiors with a fresh twist

What four designers would you like to invite to dinner?
Georges Geffroy, Renzo Mongiardino, Sister Parish, and Stéphane Boudin

What would your perfect room look like?
Jane Wrightsman's Palm Beach living room

What's your best budget-friendly design hack?
Batik bedspreads used as upholstery, tablecloths, and lampshades

What's the simplest and best design rule?
Incorporate pattern

What's a design risk worth taking?
Pattern

Tell us ways that you've used lighting to resolve a dark room.
Place it everywhere. You can always dim the lights but you cannot create light where it does not exist.

Where do you go for inspiration?

Travel, my book collection, and the Metropolitan Museum of Art

How do you make your home feel welcoming?
Flowers and candles

How do you solve your storage problems?
Donate to ARF Thrift Shop or sell

Do you really need all that stuff you have in storage?
No

Any preferences when it comes to your bed linens?
No wrinkled bed linens!

How do you design around your pets?
Create miniature furniture. We also had a powder room fitted with built-in storage (for storing pet supplies such as wee-wee pads).

What do you covet but can't afford?
To live in Versailles. It's a lot of maintenance.

What have you broken that you still mourn?
I don't believe in mourning broken things, and we work with great restorers who can fix anything.

What's the best way to start the day?
A kiss from our dog

Long hot soak in the tub or quick shower?
Quick shower

What job would you be terrible at?
Anything repetitive. Maybe a tollbooth operator;
I'd chat with everyone.

What kind of music do you listen to at home?
Sirius XM Studio 54 Radio

What smells of home for you?
NEST Candles, scented in grapefruit

What's your weekend routine?
Spending time in the Hamptons with my family and
friends, always entertaining houseguests, playing
tennis, and having dinner either out or at home.

How long can you go without tidying up?
Not long . . . at all!

**How do you make sure you enjoy your own
parties?**
Relax and always stay calm. Like I say: "When the
first guest arrives, stop fussing, relax, and enjoy."

**How do you subtly let guests know you want
them to leave?**
Yawn

How do you stock a perfect bar?
Artisanal tonics and ginger ale, Veuve Clicquot
champagne, 25-year-old Scotch, great tequila, a variety of vodkas for different tastes, my favorite rum.

What's your favorite cocktail?
Veuve Clicquot rosé champagne on ice

What's the best thing about living in New York?
I'm a born and raised New Yorker and can't imagine
living anywhere else—it's home.

What's the worst thing about living in New York?
The noise!

What do you hope never changes in New York?
Bergdorf Goodman on 57th and 5th

**What small thing makes a bad New York
day better?**
A Sant Ambroeus coffee

How do you get around town?
Uber

**Is there a particular place in the city that has a
special meaning for you?**
Decoration & Design Building. It's like home.

Teddie, Papachristidis and Nelson's adored
Yorkshire terrier, vying for attention

229

John Barman

CONTEMPORARY AND COLORFUL

Above: The walls of Barman's living room, lacquered in a neutral gray, provide a quiet backdrop to the sleek glamour of the midcentury furnishings. **Opposite:** The boxy dimensions of the dining room are counterbalanced by a coffered ceiling painted in a high-gloss yellow—intended to create the illusion of a higher ceiling—and an oversize round table.

John Barman's sophisticated renovation of his Park Avenue apartment is colorful and "swanky"—his own wonderful word for it—but it's also very refined. It's glamorous! "What's wrong with a little glamour?" he says. "It's not like you get up in the morning and it's a problem."

Barman got his first degree in business from the Wharton School of Finance at the University of Pennsylvania. He went on to study interior design in part because his mother was a decorator and he was fascinated by her career path. But was his mother interested in his input? "No."

He lives with his partner, Kelly Graham, who is also the creative design director of Barman's firm. The apartment is very large for just two people, but Barman stresses that it's important to actually use the rooms rather than allow them to become empty, formal spaces. To that end, the couple prefer to entertain at home rather than go to restaurants. "People are so surprised to be invited to someone's apartment." They serve simple food such as baked salmon and salads, and buy dessert, because Barman finds that people don't care that much about the food as long as they're having fun. The only problem is that in New York, guests leave so early. "The minute you put the dessert fork down, they're out the door."

Downtime is spent watching movies on a huge wall-mounted projection screen in the media room. And then there is the fabulous cobalt-blue lacquered library full of beautiful design books to delve into—the blue exemplifies Barman's confident use of color, which for many people can be a problem, or at least somewhat daunting. But he is not sure why, and points out that color has historically been so important—even recent decades such as the 1950s, '60s, and '80s were colorful, he reminds us. "Then all of a sudden, in the '90s, everything became beige."

Above: To accommodate more seating for entertaining, Barman divided the expansive living room into three distinct spaces and then tied it all together with tangerine, raspberry, and yellow accents. On the far wall, an abstract work by Karin Davie hangs above an L-shaped sofa. Colorful Blenko and Venini glass objects are arranged on top of the marble-and-chrome coffee table. **Left:** A highly reflective room divider with a pattern of convex spherical forms speaks to the bold geometry of the room.

Right: Black-and-silver abstract wallpaper on the ceiling of the bar area echoes the floor tiles and brushed stainless-steel cabinets. **Below:** In the library, as a transition between the dining room and front gallery, Barman chose to cover the walls in a bright cobalt-blue lacquer. A painting by Lisa Milroy hangs above a custom sofa covered in blue flannel from Loro Piana. Midcentury swivel chairs are upholstered in Mongolian lamb fur; vintage plaster-and-gold-leaf table lamps stand on sculptural metal-and-glass side tables by Paul Ferrante.

Right: Combining two apartments allowed for the creation of an oversize entrance hall that serves as a gallery for Barman's collection of contemporary art. A painting by Barnaby Furnas hangs opposite *Omertà* by Norbert Bisky.

Left: Strong clean lines, shiny surfaces, and luxury materials are the main elements in the design of this apartment. In the immaculate kitchen, custom white cabinetry is paired with Zebrino marble, giving only a hint of color to the otherwise all-white space. **Above:** In the master bathroom, an iron-legged vintage cabinet in red, white, and black laminate continues the glamorous geometry of the whole apartment.

Above: Barman chose a dramatic approach to the master bedroom with shiny black paint and mirrored walls. A painting by Kelly Stuart Graham hangs above a custom bed outfitted in linens from E. Braun & Co. The vintage night tables are from Herman Miller. **Left:** A Lucite chair from Plexi-Craft and a desk by Pierre Guariche are positioned on top of deep red wall-to-wall carpeting. A painting by Claude Venard plays off the bedroom colors.

Q+A

with John Barman

In a few words, describe your design style.
My design style is contemporary and colorful. It is always functional and comfortable and designed for the client's needs.

What designers would you like to invite to dinner?
I would have liked to have had dinner with Stéphane Boudin from Jansen, Henri Samuel, and Dorothy Draper, who has been a big influence on me.

What would your perfect room look like?
My perfect room would be all red. I designed an all-red media room, and it is fantastic.

What's your best budget-friendly design hack?
The Nix Color Sensor is an app for your mobile phone that uses a Bluetooth scanner to identify colors and is amazingly helpful. It can match any color to a real paint color.

What's the simplest and best design rule?
Function comes first. People have to live in the spaces you create, and the design should follow.

What's a design risk worth taking?
It's always worth taking a chance with bolder colors.

Tell us ways that you've used lighting to resolve a dark room.
Ceiling cove lights with LED lighting give a wonderful glow to a dark apartment.

How do you make your home feel welcoming?
By opening the curtains and shades and opening the windows and adding fresh flowers

Where do you go for inspiration?
Travel is inspiring, especially Morocco. France is always inspiring, but I can be inspired by many places—a trip to Peru was inspiring last spring but you can get inspiration closer to home, for instance at the Metropolitan Museum of Art.

What truly gives a home "life"?
A pet gives a house joy and life, but you can also add life by opening the window for fresh air and adding fresh flowers like tulips or even carnations, which last a long time.

How do you solve your storage problems?
I have a lot of closets so it's important to keep them neat and organized and continually throw out what will never be used.

Do you really need all that stuff you have in storage?
Of course—you never know what will come in handy.

Any preferences when it comes to your bed linens?
I like to have the bed look good during the day but be comfortable at night. Since I like to sleep in a cold room, it requires a lot of putting blankets away.

How do you design around your pets?
Patterned rugs are wonderful for people with pets.

What do you covet but can't afford?
A custom-designed private jet

What have you broken that you still mourn?
I get very attached to my possessions so I mourn every loss.

What's the best way to start the day?
Wake up with the curtains open and see the light and the New York City skyline—even if it is just rooftops and a bit of sky.

What's the first thing you do when you come home from a trip?
Open the curtains and the shades and the mail.

What's your weekend routine?
If I'm in the city on a weekend I go to museums and gallery exhibitions and also explore parts of the city—I've recently been to Dumbo and loved it.

Where is your favorite place to take a nap?
I can nap any place but prefer to nap on a sofa rather than my bed, so when I wake up I know it was a nap.

How do you make sure you enjoy your own parties?
Careful preparation in advance makes parties more fun for the host, along with fun guests, great music, and low lighting.

How do you subtly let guests know you want them to leave?
I'm glad to have guests stay on, which means they are having a good time.

How do you stock a perfect bar?
Since my last name is Barman, I always stock a great bar. A perfect bar is stocked with colorful bottles, whether they be filled with waters or liquors, and mixed with wonderful bar accessories—a great vintage ice bucket and ice tongs, and wonderful mixing tools with a cool bar cloth make it very stylish.

What's your favorite cocktail?
A dry martini with olives

What's the best thing about living in New York?
New York is the best place to live—the excitement, the pace, and the pulse are the best things about the city.

How do you get around town?
If it's too far to walk, I take the subway.

What do you hope never changes in New York?
Central Park. It is amazing just as it is.

Barman and Graham's sweet pug, Buster, pictured here at fifteen years old